IN THE SHADOW
OF THE SPHINX

sphinx: (Greek Mythology) 'a winged monster having the head of a woman and the body of a lion that destroyed all who could not answer its riddle'

—The American Heritage Dictionary of the English Language, New College Edition

(Note: The sphinx is an internationally recognized icon of intelligence agencies whose major activities are conducted "in the shadows")

IN THE SHADOW
OF THE SPHINX

*A New Look Into The Bay of Pigs
and JFK Assassination*

Frank R. Durr, DPA

To order additional copies of this book, contact:
Xlibris Corporation
1-888-795-4274
www.Xlibris.com
Orders@Xlibris.com
38898

CONTENTS

PART 1: THE BAY OF PIGS

PART II: ASSASSINATION OF JFK

Dedication

This book is respectfully dedicated to the courageous men and women in the intelligence community who are called upon daily to risk their lives in service to our country. And to those especially who gave it up.

Former CIA Director Richard Helms
with Author November 1999
(Photo first published in *The Intelligencer,* Winter/Spring 2005)

Preface

I have written this book for two reasons: *First*, to provide the reader with my take on the "why" and "who" in one of the greatest Unsolved mysteries of the Twentieth Century; the assassination of President John F. Kennedy. Secondly, to argue that the Bay of Pigs invasion and its subsequent failure was the product of the decision-making style of JFK ie: *Failure was the objective!*

In regard to the assassination of President Kennedy, scores of books, movies, and articles have been produced attempting to (or in some way) to shed light on the event specifically on the "who" and "why". While many have contained some element of truth (or Fact), none of them have identified the "whom". *That is why this book is different!* This is not to say that Kennedy did not want rid of Castro. He did! (I will cite examples). I will also argue that there was a connection between the assassination of JFK and South Vietnam's President Diem. I will provide the reader with a "person of interest" whom I believe was a major player in the conspiracy.

Another difference between *this book* and the "pack" is that I believe that I am the only writer in the field who has personal knowledge of a group that claimed *responsibility* for JFK's assassination! In 1964, in (then) West Germany, I came into possession of this information when I was assigned to the 66th Military Intelligence Group (US Army) in Schweinfurt, West Germany. Here again, is an example of why this book differs from all of the others; I was not looking for the killer(s), I was searching for information that would substantiate the group's claim of responsibility. In *this book*, I offer the reader the results of my search ie: The "best evidence" that I have uncovered. In order to make my findings to the reader as clear as possible, I have decided to write it in two parts (I and II).

In Part I, I present my "take" on the Bay of Pigs operation. I examine the planning, the confusion, certain elements of the operation, and the doubts about the mission from its very conception. The method that I have chosen to advance my argument is to offer *A List of Findings* followed by a discussion of each finding. (Part II, The Assassination of President Kennedy, will follow the same Format).

In Part II, I will add to the "mix" of theories relative to the Assassination, a critical piece of information, which is, as far as I know, information that I alone have been privy to since 1964. When first became aware of this "new" intelligence, I immediately filed a classified report and "passed" it up the intelligence "chain of command". What happened after that, I do not know. In my opinion, it was probably ignored since it was believed to be inconceivable that the group claiming responsibility could have possibly been involved. However, in light of the information that I will present in this book, I believe that I can make the case that this group could have shot the president. Of course, they could not have done it alone. I will not only offer a motive, but also an individual who could have orchestrated the entire operation from beginning to end.

Finally, *a word of warning*. As you proceed through the ensuing chapters, try to keep an open mind; beware of "conventional thinking". The "Cult of Intelligence" is, more often than not, a dark, secretive world full of hidden meanings, where "things" are not always as they seem to be; where black is white and where lies are more important than truth. On *this* warning, *this* author *knows* where of he writes.

Author's Notes: In order to create a better understanding for the reader, "author's notes" will be used throughout the book to offer insight, opinions, explanations, clarification, amplification, or to call attention to something previously mentioned.

LIST OF FINDINGS

In The Case of The Bay of Pigs Investigation

1. That the original plan submitted by the CIA and approved by President Eisenhower, in 1960, was a plan to depose Castro patterned after the highly successful "Guatemala Model" carried out by the CIA, in 1954, to depose Guatemalan Presi- dent Jacobo Arbenz.
2. That shortly after his election in November, 1960, Presi- dent-Elect Kennedy was briefed on the operation by Allen Dulles. However, unknown to him, the plan that had been approved by Eisenhower, had been drastically revamped and no resemblance to the Guatemala Model.
3. That from the very instant that Kennedy was briefed on the operation by Dulles, he had grave reservations about its chance of success. Never-the-less, he gave the CIA permis- sion to finalize the plan with the understanding that under no circumstances would any US military be involved.
4. That immediately after assuming office in January, 1961, pressure began building for him to set the operation in motion. Faced with a political dilemma of monumental proportions, the President allowed the operation to go forward after assurances from Dulles that it would be successful without any intervention of US military forces.
5. That from the very beginning, the President realized that the operation was fatally flawed and took steps to insure its failure. In the process, he avoided a confrontation with the Soviet Union.

PART 1

The Bay of Pigs

"The importance of a decision is not how much it costs, but how quickly it can be reversed if it is wrong"

—Peter Drucker

"But the doubts of Rusk* and Fulbright** and of others were all the while imper- ceptibly converging on the President and, bit by bit, an operation that was marginal to begin with was so truncated as to guarantee its failure."

—Charles J.V. Murphy
Fortune Magazine

---

*   Dean Rusk, Secretary of State
**   Sen. William Fulbright, Chairman, Senate Foreign Relations Committee

Introduction

Much has been written about the Bay of Pigs fiasco. All of the accounts that have read either blame its failure of the operation on the President or the CIA. For many years, the "either/or conclusions were "good enough" for myself and, for most Americans. After all, in retrospect, the whole operation was just a "blip" on the screen of world events during the Cold War, or . . . Was it? Is it possible that the Bay of Pigs failure was really a major political victory for the Kennedy Administration that ranks high on a scale along side of the political victory the President achieved in the Cuban Missile Crisis? My opinion may be in the minority but I believe that it does!

In 1975, about a year and a half after I retired from the US Army, I obtained a job with Florida's Department of Health and Rehabilitative Services (HRS), in Tampa, Florida. It was while I was with HRS that I first met someone who had actually participated in the Bay of Pigs invasion. We were brought together by a co-worker of mine, who had been married to "Pepe" (as I will call him). One afternoon when we were having lunch she casually mentioned that she had been married to a "high-ranking" officer" who had been a member of the Cuban Brigade, had participated in the invasion, been captured and ransomed back after a year in captivity. All of a sudden, a routine lunch break became an important event. When I began To press her for more information about Pepe, she told me that he never spoke about his ordeal but she promised to ask him if he would talk with me about it. As it turned out, Pepe was en employee of HRS and working out of our Tampa office.

Within a few days, my friend told me that Pepe had agreed to talk with me. The meeting took place on a hot summer afternoon outside the old HRS building in downtown Tampa. From the very beginning, it was obvious that Pepe was extremely bitter about the whole operation from beginning to end. During the entire conversation, he rarely, ever looked directly at me but rather alternated from talking with his head lower toward the ground to talking while gazing in the distance. This coupled with the din of afternoon traffic, made hearing very difficult. Never the less, I was sure that this would be my only opportunity to talk with this man. To compensate, I moved in as close to him but not so close as to disturb him. (As I mentioned, it was a hot sunny afternoon but the atmosphere around Pepe was definitely "chilly" and I felt it). What follows are my recollections of his story:

Pepe, a member of the Batista army was forced to flee Cuba when Castro took over the Island. When he learned about the planned liberation of Cuba, he was one of the first to volunteer. His induction to the brigade took plane in South Florida. Later, he was moved between Guatemala, Puerto Rico, and Nicaragua. He recalled that the training was haphazard and often chaotic. There were many days when there was no training and nothing to do; the men lounged around, restless, waiting for the CIA instructors to begin training. Fistfights were common and discipline was non-existent. Living conditions for the Cubans were often unbearable; a shortage of housing, cots, bedclothes, sanitary and bathing facilities, food, water, clothes and ammunition was common. Morale suffered. Factionalism among the brigade added to the confusion. The result was a poorly trained, poorly equipped brigade. Even so, when the order came to begin the invasion, members of the brigade were jubilant. With the promised air and naval support of the US, Cuba would be liberated. As it turned out, the promises were all lies. Pepe, a Battalion Commander, never reached shore to fight the enemy; his ship was hit and most of his men killed or drown. Pepe was "lucky" he eventually made it to shore and was immediately captured.

When I asked Pepe how the operation could have turned out so badly, he replied, "*Because it was designed to fail!*" In retrospect, Pepe's statement, while shocking at the time, has been borne out by many researchers and historians. As an investigator, I began to study the operation from a point of view that the failure could be something more than the result of "pee-poor" plans, poorly executed. I began to explore the possibility that there was a force at work, which was *designed* and implemented from the time that Kennedy took office, intentional, if you will, to accomplish a greater "good". Of course, it remains for the reader to decide if I have made my case.

Chapter One

That the original plan submitted by the CIA and approved by President Eisenhower, in 1960, was a plan to depose Castro patterned after the highly successful "Guatemala Model" carried out by the CIA, in 1954, to depose of Guatemalan President Jacobo Arbenz.

I begin this segment of the *Bay of Pigs* with the question: Where did the idea of deposing Castro originate? A study of the history of Cuba reveals continuing political and economic strife usually ending in revolution. For the most part, the United States Government has maintained over the years, a "hands-off" policy regarding Cuba, that is, until Castro came to power. In the beginning, when Castro began his struggle against the dictator, Batiste, he was hailed as a hero in this country. However, soon after his victory, it became clear to most Americans, especially those with business interests on the Island, that Castro represented a political and economic threat to this country.

When Batiste was overthrown, thousands of his partisans fled to this country. Most settled in the Miami, Florida area. Soon after Castro took control of the government, he made it clear that he was going to institute socialist reform throughout the Island. This triggered a "second wave" of Cubans who did not want to live in a socialist society. Many of those in this wave of refugees had supported Castro and the revolution, including many from his guerrilla forces who had fought at Castro's side in the isolated mountain areas of Cuba. Most in this group also settled in South Florida.

Author's Notes: It is important to remember that there was a vast political divide between the first sand second wave of refugees; the first came to be known as "Batistes". Many of these were considered to still have ties to the ousted dictator. Within the second wave were many who were considered "Castroites", those who were thought to support Castro but not socialist government. This resulted in deep-seated distrust between the two camps that most likely remains to this day.

/-/-/-/-/-/-/-/-/

In the meantime, the mass exodus of Cubans from the Island did not seem to bother Castro at all. While he was pursuing Socialist reforms, he was, at the same time, inviting a few known members of the Communist Party to become part of his government.

As Castro consolidated his control of the Island, he began to nationalize businesses belonging to foreign investors, in particular, American business interests. Among those confiscated were Sears Roebuck, General Electric, Coca Cola, and the United Fruit Company (UFC) which own huge tracks of land in Cuba. Hotels were also nationalized including the Havana Hilton (renamed the Havana Libre)

Another priority of Castro was to develop a well-trained and refurbished military organization. Knowing that he could not expect any help from the United States, he made friendly overtures to the Soviets. Initially, the Soviets were unsure about Castro's intentions. After all, no Cuban government had ever recognized the government of the Soviet Union. Never the less, Khrushchev, then Premier of the Soviet Union, decided to take the risk and responded to Castro's overtures in the form of economic and military aid. To their surprise and delight, Castro accepted their offer and the Soviets immediately opened diplomatic relations with Cuba.

That reality that a Soviet Satellite could be just 90 miles off the Coast of the United States alarmed the Central Intelligence Agency (CIA). In response to the threat, Allen Dulles, CIA Director, asked for, and got, a meeting with President Eisenhower to brief him on the situation and discuss some options that might be taken to deal with the situation. According to Peter Wyden (*Bay of Pigs: The Untold Story*), "The President was sympathetic but his interest was routine. Acts of sabotage that could be carried out by the CIA were considered inadequate by both men. Then, the President told Dulles if he and his people really wanted to mount a greater effort, they should come back with a program". *1* Thus, the invasion plan to depose Castro was set in motion.

Who *actually* developed the plan remains somewhat within the shadow of the CIA. What is known is that the original plan, the one that was submitted to President Eisenhower, was based on the highly successful *Guatemalan Model*. In 1954, the CIA, along with a few "rag-tag" soldiers, a few aircraft, and a successful propaganda campaign, overthrew a "duly elected" Guatemalan President, Jacobo Arbenz (Guzman) who had made the mistake of attacking the United Fruit Company. (UFC). Why, you might ask, would the Guatemalan President's attack on the United Fruit Company create the need for the CIA to topple his regime? Since the beginning of the 20th Century, when the UFC acquired massive chunks of land in Guatemala for its fruit-growing industry,

Re: 1. *Bay of Pigs: The Untold Story*, by Peter Wyden, Simon & Schuster, New York, 1979

the company's geo-expansion in that area, and its resulting involvement and influence on US policy towards Central America, led to the appellation of that part of the world as the "Banana Republic".

Just how "cozy" did the United Fruit Company get with the US Government in 1954? For "openers", *John Foster Dulles*, then the Secretary of State, was the former member of a New York City law firm that represented the United Fruit Company. *Allen Dulles*, then Director of Central Intelligence Agency (and brother of the Secretary of State), was a former member of the UFC Board of Trustees. Even before 1954, members of the United Fruit Company were involved with the US Government. During WWII, "Wild Bill" Donovan, the legendary head of the Office of Strategic Services (OSS), a clandestine organization (the precursor of the CIA), recruited a former advertising director of the UFC as his envoy to the Middle East.

Having made the case (I believe) that the United Fruit Company was heavily "entwined" in the US policy in Central America, the question of "why" the CIA took action against the Arbenz Government can be readily understood. When Arbenz was elected, one of his first actions was to confiscate all of the holdings and land owned by the United Fruit Company and divided it among the peasant farmers.

Author's Notes: If you don't already know, did you ever wonder why the Central Intelligence Agency is nicknamed, "The Company"? When the CIA was first formed; its mission was to destabilize foreign governments whose interests were inimical to our own. As it turned out, the agency became entangled with the governments whose *business* interests were deemed inimical to American businesses, especially in Central America with UFC and the "Banana Republic". Hence, the nickname, "The Company".

/-/-/-/-/-/-/-/-/

When Castro took over power in Cuba, he must have been well aware of what happened to Arbenz in Guatemala. One cannot overlook the fact that he was both an intellectual and a brilliant strategist. The stage is now set. To recap:

1. Castro has successfully overthrown Batista and has moved to consolidate his grip on the Island and instituted a Socialist form of government including known Communists.

2. In the process, he has confiscated all properties of the United Fruit Company and nationalized all North American business interests. Thousands flee to South Florida.
3. He has entered into an agreement with the Soviets to provide him with economic and military support.
4. In response to the threat, Allen Dulles, Director of Central Intelligence has met with President Eisenhower to brief him on the situation and get his approval to develop a plan to remove Castro.

On March 17, 1960, Dulles submitted a plan to Eisenhower, which he approved. The plan is attached as Exhibit 1-1. However, due to the poor quality of the copy, I am offering its contents below (Courtesy of the Eisenhower Library):

> "This document is our basic policy paper. It was approved by the President at a meeting in the White House on March 17, 1960"

A PROGRAM OF COVERT ACTION AGAINST THE CASTRO REGIME

1. *Objective*: The purpose of the program outlined herein is to bring about the replacement of the Castro regime with one more devoted to the true interests of the Cuban people, and more acceptable to the U.S., in such a manner as to avoid any appearance of U.S. intervention. Essentially, the method of accomplishing this end will be to induce, support, and so far as possible direct action, both inside and outside Cuba, by select groups of Cubans of a sort that might be expected to and could undertake on their own initiative. Since a crisis inevitably entailing drastic action in or toward Cuba could be provoked by circumstances beyond control of the U.S. before the covert action program has accomplished its objective, every effort will be made to carry it out in such a way as progressively to improve the capacity of the U.S. to act in a crisis.

2. *Summary Outline*: The program contemplates four major courses of action:

    a. The first requirement is the creation of a responsible, appealing and unified Cuban opposition to the Castro regime publicly declared as such and therefore necessarily located outside of Cuba. It is hoped that within one month a political entity can be formed in the shape of a council or junta, through the merger of three acceptable opposition groups with which the Central Intelligence Agency is already in contact. The council will be encouraged to adopt as its slogan "Restore the Revolution", to develop a political position consistent with tat slogan, and to address itself to the Cuban people as an attractive political alternative to Castro. This vocal opposition will: serve as a magnet for the loyalties of the Cubans; in actuality conduct and direct various opposition activities; and provide cover for other compartmented CIA controlled operations. (Exhibit 1—Tab A)

b. So that the opposition may be heard and Castro's basis of popular support undermined, it is necessary to develop the means for mass communication to the Cuban people so that a powerful propaganda offensive can be initiated in the name of declared opposition. The major tool proposed to be used for this purpose is a long and short wave gray broadcasting facility, probably to be located on Swan Island. The target date for its completion is two months. This will be supplemented by broadcasting from U.S. commercial facilities paid for by private Cuban groups and by the clandestine distribution of written material inside the country. (Exhibit 1—Tab B)

Author's Notes: The propaganda offensive was to be coordinated by David Atlee Phillips, a high-profile operative of the CIA in Central America. His propaganda efforts were considered critical to the success of the "Guatemala Model". With reference to the phrase "long and short wave gray broadcasting facility; it is a radio station operating "in the open" but operating for a specific intelligence purpose.

/-/-/-/-/-/-/-/-/

c. Work is already in progress in the creation of a covert intelligence and action organization in Cuba, which will be responsive to the orders and directions for the "exile" opposition. Such a network must have effective communication and be selectively manned to minimize the risk of penetration. An effective organization can probably be created within 60 days. Its role will be to provide hard intelligence and exfiltration of individuals, to assist in the internal distribution of illegal propaganda, and to plan and organize for the defection of key individuals and groups as directed.

d. Preparations have already been made for the development of an adequate paramilitary force outside Cuba, together with mechanisms for the necessary logistic support of covert military operations on the Island. Initially, a cadre of leaders will be recruited after careful screening and trained as paramilitary instructors. In a second phase, a number of paramilitary cadres will be trained to secure locations outside of the U.S. so as to be available for immediate deployment into Cuba to organize, train, and lead resistance forces recruited there both before and after the establishment of one or more active centers of resistance. The creation of this capability will require a minimum of six months and probably closer to eight. In the meanwhile, a limited air capability for resupply and for infiltration already exists under CIA control and can be rather easily expanded if and when the situation requires. Within two months it is hoped to parallel this with a small air resupply capability under deep cover as a commercial operation in another country.

3. *Leadership*: It is important to avoid distracting and divisive rivalry among the outstanding Cuban opposition leaders for the senior role in the opposition. Accordingly, every effort will be made to have an eminent, non-ambitious, politically uncontentious chairman selected. The emergence of a successor to Castro becomes more imminent, the senior leader must be elected, U.S. support focused upon him, and his build up undertaken.

4. *Cover*: All actions undertaken by CIA in support and on behalf of the opposition council will, of course, be explained as activities of that entity (insofar as the actions become publicly at all). The CIA will, however, have to have direct contacts with a certain number of Cubans and, to protect these, will make use of a carefully screened Group of U.S. businessmen with a stated interest in Cuban affairs and desire to support the opposition. They will act as a funding

mechanism and channel for guidance and support to the directorate of the opposition under controlled conditions. CIA personnel will be as representatives of this group. In order to strengthen the cover, it is hoped that substantial funds can be raised from private sources to support the opposition. $100,000 has already been pledged from U.S. sources. At an appropriate time, a bond issue will be floated by the council (as an obligation on a future Cuban government) to raise an additional $2,000,000.

5. *Budget*: (Readers can find the budget in Exhibit 1—Tab C)
6. *Recommendations*: That the Central Intelligence Agency be authorized to undertake the above outlined program and to with draw the funds required for this purpose as set forth in paragraph 5. from the Agency's Reserve for contingencies.

Author's Notes: Tab A and B are recommended reading and are attached to the "original" copy (Exhibit 1). The program, outlined above, is a "repeat" of the Guatemalan Model that worked so well against Arbenz. For those readers with an intelligence background, I am sure that you will recognize the "program" as one that follows a customary genre for proposed intelligence operations. During my tour in Vietnam, I read many such plans as well as help write some of type of "formula" plans.

EYES ONLY
~~SECRET~~

This document is our basic policy
paper. It was approved by the
President at a meeting in the
White House on 17 March 1960.

[Copy of original plan to depose Castro: submitted to
and approved by President
Eisenhower. dtd 17Mar60]

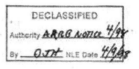
EYES ONLY
~~SECRET~~

EXHIBIT 1

A PROGRAM OF COVERT ACTION AGAINST THE CASTRO REGIME

1. **Objective:** The purpose of the program outlined herein is to bring about the replacement of the Castro regime with one more devoted to the true interests of the Cuban people and more acceptable to the U.S. in such a manner as to avoid any appearance of U.S. intervention. Essentially the method of accomplishing this end will be to induce, support, and so far as possible direct action, both inside and outside of Cuba, by selected groups of Cubans of a sort that they might be expected to and could undertake on their own initiative. Since a crisis inevitably entailing drastic action in or toward Cuba could be provoked by circumstances beyond control of the U.S. before the covert action program has accomplished its objective, every effort will be made to carry it out in such a way as progressively to improve the capability of the U.S. to act in a crisis.

2. **Summary Outline:** The program contemplates four major courses of action:

   a. The first requirement is the creation of a responsible, appealing and unified Cuban opposition to the Castro regime, publicly declared as such and therefore necessarily located outside of Cuba. It is hoped that within one month a political entity can be formed in the shape of a council or junta, through the merger of three acceptable opposition groups with which the Central Intelligence Agency is already in contact. The council will be encouraged to adopt as its slogan "Restore the

Revolution", to develop a political position consistent with that slogan, and to address itself to the Cuban people as an attractive political alternative to Castro. This vocal opposition will: serve as a magnet for the loyalties of the Cubans; in actuality conduct and direct various opposition activities; and provide cover for other compartmented CIA controlled operations. (Tab A)

b. So that the opposition may be heard and Castro's basis of popular support undermined, it is necessary to develop the means for mass communication to the Cuban people so that a powerful propaganda offensive can be initiated in the name of the declared opposition. The major tool proposed to be used for this purpose is a long and short wave gray broadcasting facility, probably to be located on Swan Island. The target date for its completion is two months. This will be supplemented by broadcasting from U.S. commercial facilities paid for by private Cuban groups and by the clandestine distribution of written material inside the country. (Tab B)

c. Work is already in progress in the creation of a covert intelligence and action organization within Cuba which will be responsive to the orders and directions of the "exile" opposition. Such a network must have effective communication and be selectively manned to minimize the risk of penetration. An effective organization can probably be created within 60 days. Its role will be to provide hard

intelligence, to arrange for the illegal infiltration and exfiltration
of individuals, to assist in the internal distribution of illegal
propaganda, and to plan and organize for the defection of key individuals
and groups as directed.

d. Preparations have already been made for the development of
an adequate paramilitary force outside of Cuba, together with mechanisms
for the necessary logistic support of covert military operations on
the Island. Initially a cadre of leaders will be recruited after careful screening and trained as paramilitary instructors. In a second
phase a number of paramilitary cadres will be trained at secure locations
outside of the U.S. so as to be available for immediate deployment into
Cuba to organize, train and lead resistance forces recruited there both
before and after the establishment of one or more active centers of
resistance. The creation of this capability will require a minimum of
six months and probably closer to eight. In the meanwhile, a limited
air capability for resupply and for infiltration and exfiltration already
exists under CIA control and can be rather easily expanded if and when
the situation requires. Within two months it is hoped to parallel this
with a small air resupply capability under deep cover as a commercial
operation in another country.

3. Leadership: It is important to avoid distracting and devisive rivalry
among the outstanding Cuban opposition leaders for the senior role in the

opposition. Accordingly, every effort will be made to have an eminent, non-ambitious, politically uncontentious chairman selected. The emergence of a successor to Castro should follow careful assessment of the various personalities active in the opposition to identify the one who can attract, control, and lead the several forces. As the possibility of an overthrow of Castro becomes more imminent, the senior leader must be selected, U.S. support focused upon him, and his build up undertaken.

4. Cover: All actions undertaken by CIA in support and on behalf of the opposition council will, of course, be explained as activities of that entity (insofar as the actions become publicly known at all). The CIA will, however, have to have direct contacts with a certain number of Cubans and, to protect these, will make use of a carefully screened group of U.S. businessmen with a stated interest in Cuban affairs and desire to support the opposition. They will act as a funding mechanism and channel for guidance and support to the directorate of the opposition under controlled conditions. CIA personnel will be documented as representatives of this group. In order to strengthen the cover it is hoped that substantial funds can be raised from private sources to support the opposition. $100,000 has already been pledged from U.S. sources. At an appropriate time a bond issue will be floated by the council (as an obligation on a future Cuban government) to raise an additional $2,000,000.

5. Budget: It is anticipated that approximately $4,409,000 of CIA funds will be required for the above program. On the assumption that it will not

reach its culmination earlier than 6 to 8 months from now, the estimated requirements for FY-1960 funds is $900,000 with the balance of $3,500,000 required in FY-1961. The distribution of costs between fiscal years could, of course, be greatly altered by policy decisions or unforeseen contingencies which compelled accelerated paramilitary operations. (Tab C)

6. Recommendations: That the Central Intelligence Agency be authorized to undertake the above outlined program and to withdraw the funds required for this purpose as set forth in paragraph 5. from the Agency's Reserve for contingencies.

EYES ONLY

~~SECRET~~

THE POLITICAL OPPOSITION

1. CIA is already in close touch with three reputable opposition groups (the Montecristi, Autentico Party and the National Democratic Front). These all meet the fundamental criteria conditional to acceptance, i.e. they are for the revolution as originally conceived--many being former 26th of July members--and are not identified with either Batista or Trujillo. They are anti-Castro because of his failure to live up to the original 26th of July platform and his apparent willingness to sell out to Communist domination and possible ultimate enslavement. These groups, therefore, fit perfectly the planned opposition slogan of "Restore the Revolution".

2. An opposition Council or Junta will be formed within 30 days from representatives of these groups augmented possibly by representatives of other groups. It is probably premature to have a fixed platform for the Council but the Caracas Manifesto of 20 July 1958 contains a number of exploitable points. Two of the CIA group leaders were signers of the Manifesto. The following points are suggested as a few possibilities:

   a. The Castro regime is the new dictatorship of Cuba subject to strong Sino-Soviet influence.

   b. Cuba is entitled to an honest, democratic government based on free elections. There is no hope of this as long as Castro throttles the rights of legitimate political parties and the freedom of expression.

EYES ONLY

~~SECRET~~

c. A realistic agrarian reform program providing for individual ownership of the land must be put into effect.

d. Individual freedoms must be restored and collectivism in commerce and education must be eliminated.

e. Sino-Soviet influence in the affairs of Cuba must be eliminated. A special research group of Cubans with American support is planned to refine and expand these planks and to produce propaganda materials based on the above platform for use by and on behalf of the opposition Council.

EYES ONLY
~~SECRET~~

PROPAGANDA

1. Articulation and transmission of opposition views has already begun. Private opposition broadcasts (i.e. purchase of commercial time by private individuals) have occurred in Miami (medium wave) and arrangements have been made with Station WRUL for additional broadcasts from Massachusetts (short wave) and Florida (broadcast band). Presidents Betancourt and Ydigoras have also agreed to the use of commercial stations for short wave broadcasts from Caracas and Guatemala City. CIA has furnished support to these efforts through encouragement, negotiating help and providing some broadcast material.

2. As the major voice of the opposition, it is proposed to establish at least one "gray" U.S.-controlled station. This will probably be on Swan Island and will employ both high frequency and broadcast band equipment of substantial power. The preparation of scripts will be done in the U.S. and these will be transmitted electronically to the site for broadcasting. After some experience and as the operation progresses, it may be desirable to supplement the Swan Island station with at least one other to ensure fully adequate coverage of all parts of Cuba, most especially the Havana region. Such an additional facility might be installed on a U.S. base in the Bahamas or temporary use might be made of a shipborne station if it is desired to avoid "gray" broadcasting from Florida.

EYES ONLY
~~SECRET~~

3. Newspapers are also being supported and further support is planned for the future. Avance, a leading Cuban daily (Zayas' paper), has been confiscated as has El Mundo, another Cuban daily. Diario de la Marina, one of the hemisphere's outstanding conservative dailies published in Havana, is having difficulty and may have to close soon. Arrangements have already been made to print Avance weekly in the U.S. for introduction into Cuba clandestinely and mailing throughout the hemisphere on a regular basis. As other leading newspapers are expropriated, publication of "exile" editions will be considered.

4. Inside Cuba, a CIA-controlled action group is producing and distributing anti-Castro and anti-Communist publications regularly. CIA is in contact with groups outside Cuba who will be assisted in producing similar materials for clandestine introduction into Cuba.

5. Two prominent Cubans are on lecture tours in Latin America. They will be followed by others of equal calibre. The mission of these men will be to gain hemisphere support for the opposition to Castro. Controlled Western Hemisphere assets (press, radio, television) will support this mission as will selected American journalists who will be briefed prior to Latin American travel.

Tab C

EYES ONLY
~~SECRET~~   Bay of Pigs - 22

FINANCIAL ANNEX

		FY-1960	FY-1961
I.	**Political Action**		
	Support of Opposition Elements and other Group Activities	150,000	800,000
II.	**Propaganda**		
	Radio Operations and Programming (including establishment of transmitters)	460,000	700,000
	Press and Publications	100,000	300,000
III.	**Paramilitary**		
	In-Exfiltration Maritime and Air Support Material and Training	200,000	1,300,000
IV.	**Intelligence Collection**	50,000	200,000
	Totals	*900,000	3,500,000

*These figures are based on the assumption that major action will not occur until FY-1961. If by reason of policy decisions or other contingencies over which the Agency cannot exercise control, the action program should be accelerated, additional funds will be required.

EYES ONLY
~~SECRET~~

Chapter Two

That shortly after his election in November, 1960, President-elect Kennedy was briefed on the operation by Allen Dulles. However, unknown to him, the plan that had been approved by Eisenhower, had been drastically revamped and bore no resemblance to the Guatemala Model.

"the process is the product"

—Mary Parker Folett,
the "mother" of modern
management

The *Guatemala Model* was a simple one; train some Cuban exiles and let them infiltrate back into the Island to join other anti-Castro forces in the mountains. Landing them should be an easy task for the CIA since they had been involved in this type of operation for a number of years. As a matter-of-fact, there is considerable evidence that many of the planners thought nothing more of it than "a walk in the park". So, why deviate from the original plan?

First and foremost, I believe the fear was that the Soviet Union would turn the Island into a military fortress. In doing so, they could use Cuba as a base of operations to spread Communism throughout Central and South America. For the Soviets, the opportunity was totally unexpected. Khrushchev was later to recall "At the time that Fidel Castro led his revolution to victory and entered Havana with his troops, we had no idea what political course his regime would follow. We knew there were individual Communists participating in the movement, which Castro led, but the Communist Party of Cuba had no contact with him. The whole situation was unclear". (Re: 2) The CIA's fears were well justified. "We gave them tanks and artillery and sent them instructors. In addition, we sent them anti-aircraft guns and some fighter planes. As a result of our assistance, Cuba was solidly armed". (Re: 3)

I think that it is obvious that, almost from the very beginning, Castro expected an invasion from his powerful neighbor to the North. The only question was when and where. Oddly enough, these were the two questions that the CIA planners were unsure about! One of the contributing factors to their uncertainty was the Election of 1960. No one knew who would follow Eisenhower in to the White House. If I were guessing, I would guess that they hoped that it would be Nixon. Why? If for no other reason, Nixon was already in the "Executive Loop" and would be easier to sell the idea to. Recall for a moment that all during the '60 election campaign, Kennedy had "slammed" the Eisenhower administration for its lack of action against a Communist Cuba "just 90 miles off the coast of Florida". The truth of the matter was that Nixon *knew* about the planned operation but was constrained for security reasons from defending himself and the administration.

Re: 2. *Khrushchev Remembers*, by Nikita Khrushchev (translated by Strobe Talbot, Little, Brown and Company, 1970 (pg. 488-499)

Re: 3. Ibid. (pg. 491)

I think that there was probably another reason why the planners decided to "step—up" the operation; they believed that the time was "ripe" for the revolution in Cuba. Where did they get that idea? *They got it from the same kind of intelligence sources* that told them that the Iraqis would greet our troops with flowers and dancing in the streets! Intelligence Reports coming into the CIA painted an opportunistic picture of unrest in Cuba.

> "Opposition to the Castro regime is becoming more open. The lower classes are now actively opposed to Castro". (Re: 4)

> "The people have begun to lose their fear of the government . . . . subtle sabotage is common . . . . It is generally believed that the Cuban army . . . . will not fight". (Re: 5)

Author's Notes: I intend to revisit the idea of "misinformation" which the above intelligence reports are obviously a good example.

/-/-/-/-/-/-/-/-/

As I have already indicated, the President-elect was briefed on the operation by Allen Dulles at the Kennedy Compound in Palm Beach, Florida. According to Ted Sorensen, the Special Counsel to the new president, "When briefed on the operation by the CIA in Palm Beach, he had been astonished at its magnitude and daring. He told me (Sorensen) later that he had grave doubts from that moment on". (Re: 6) He then goes on to what the President *thought* was the plan:

1. "The President *thought* he was approving a quiet, even though large-scale rein filtration of fourteen hundred Cuban exiles back into their homeland . . .
2. The President *thought* he was approving a plan whereby the exiles, should they fail to hold and expand a beachhead, could take up guerrilla warfare with other rebels in the mountains . . .

Re: 4. IR#CS-3/469,391

Re: 5. IR#CS-3/470,587 (Wyden's *Bay of Pigs*)

Re: 6. *Kennedy* by Ted Sorensen, Harper & Rowe, 1965 (pg. 295)

3. The President *thought* he was permitting the Cuban exiles, as represented by their Revolutionary Council and brigade leaders. To decide whether to risk their own lives and liberty for the liberty of their country without any overt American support . . .
4. The President *thought* he was approving a plan calculated to succeed with the help of the Cuban underground, military desertions, and in time, an uprising of a rebellious population . . .
5. The President *thought* he was approving a plan rushed into execution on the grounds that Castro would later acquire the military capability to defeat it . . .

The President, having approved the plan with assurances that it would be both clandestine and successful, thus found, in fact, that it was too large to be clandestine, and too small to be successful. (Re: 7) In retrospect, what is widely known (now) by historians, are the *false* assumptions and the *stark* reality. For example:

1. *Assumption*: No one would know that the United States was responsible for the invasion.

    Reality: Everyone knew, even the Soviets!

2. *Assumption*: Should the exiles fail to secure a beachhead, they could join other guerrillas in the Escambray Mountains.

    Reality: The Escambray Mountains were at the other end of Cuba near the original landing site (Trinidad) n*ot* close to the Bay of Pigs landing, the alternative site (a distance of between 200-300 miles)

3. *Assumption*: The exile invasion force had high morale and were willing to carry out the operation without support from US military forces.

    Reality: Many of the exiles felt that they were poorly trained and fully expected the US military to come to their aid in the event it was needed (a promise either made *or inferred* by the planners of the operation).

4. *Assumption*: The mood of the Cuban people was ripe for rebellion and that the Cuban underground was strong enough to create chaos throughout the Island violent enough to topple Castro.

Reality: Castro, aware of the impending invasion, had cracked down on the underground rendering it useless. The mood of the Cuban people had also been grossly misjudged. This brings into serious questions the quality of intelligence that the planners had relied upon.

5. *Assumption*: Castro would soon acquire substantial military support from the Soviet Union, including ground personnel which meant putting off the invasion may put the Soviets "at-risk" creating a military confrontation between the US and the Soviet Union.

    Reality: The Soviets and the Soviet-Bloc country, Czechoslovakia, had already provided Castro with substantial ground support, weapons and ammunition to him.

The question that begs to be asked is how could the planners have been so wrong about so many assumptions? For example, the assumption that Castro would *soon* acquire military support from the Soviet Union. Tim Weiner, writing in the New York Times, 23 March 01, reported that as early as September 28, 1959, the Castro government was arranging an arms deal with the Czechs:

> "The files say the Czechs supplied Cuba with 50,000 9-millimeter guns and millions of bullets, shipped y a Swiss middleman, who said "The purchase will be financed by the American religious organization, CARE, which is apparently as part of its charity work, a major buyer of Cuban sugar'"

Author's Notes: CARE! I wonder how many of my readers have donated to CARE. Tim Weiner, in his article, "Bay of Pigs Finally Sit Down Together", *New York Times*, dated 23 Mar 01, indicates that CARE was implicated in a report of the Czech Politburo file dated Sept. 28, 1959. Just for the record, *The American Heritage Dictionary*, (New College Edition), states that CARE: "Cooperative for American Remittances Everywhere, a non profit organization set up after World War II to send packages of food and clothing to needy people overseas." Whether or not the CARE organization made any attempt to refute this article's allegation, I do not know. I made no attempt to contact them. One can almost always find "bad apples" in any nonprofit.

Re: 7. Ibid., (pgs. 302, 303)

/-/-/-/-/-/-/-/-/-/

Another reason that we lacked good intelligence on Castro and Cuba was, I believe, the fact that we underestimated the Cuban intelligence capability, i.e.: the KGB trained Direccion General de Inteligencia (DGI). In addition, I don't believe that we ever knew (until much later) how much influence the KGB exerted over the DGI and its intelligence gathering activities. Not only did they control the DGI but they also tried to control Castro! How many know, for example, that the KGB tried to depose Castro in about 1968? This was the result of Castro's refusal to remove what the KGB considered anti-Soviet members of the DGI (They eventually got their way).

Up to this point, I have used the word "planners" to identify those who were behind this Bay of Pigs Operation (as most other writers have done).

Now, I would like to call attention to those that I believe were the most influential in developing the plan (in no particular order):

Richard M. Nixon, Vice-President of the United States (1952-1960)

There is ample evidence to suggest that the Vice-President was most anxious to get rid of Castro before the 1960 election. For example, shortly after his successful overthrow of Batiste, Castro visited the US where he received a hero's welcome. When he visited Washington, Nixon was given the opportunity to interview him on behalf of Eisenhower. The interview took place on a Sunday afternoon and lasted for several hours. The interview left Nixon frustrated and provoked and was later to write that he became "the strongest and most persistent advocate for setting up and supporting" a covert military effort to unseat the man who had kept him working that afternoon. (Re: 8) True to his conviction, the Vice-President prodded the CIA to come up with such a plan to "unseat" Castro (hopefully) prior to the 1960 election.

Allen Dulles, Director of the CIA (1953-1961)

Dulles earned the title of "master spy" during his assignment in the OSS in World War II. After the war, he returned to civilian life but in 1951, at the invitation of then Director of the CIA, General Walter "Beetle" Smith, Dulles became the deputy director of operations. When Eisenhower was elected president in 1952, he appointed Dulles to head the CIA. Under Dulles, the

CIA planned and carried out the Bay of Pigs Operation. Its failure cost him his job in 1961.

Richard Bissell Jr., Chief of CIA Clandestine Service (1959-1961)

Bissell joined the CIA in 1954, as a special assistant to Dulles and quickly became his "right-hand" man. Among his early accomplishments were the successful coup of the Arbenz government in Guatemala (1954) and the development of the U-2, spy plane program. Considered by many as the next-in-line to become Director of the CIA, Bissell was given the task of toppling Castro. As such, the Bay of Pigs became "his plan". When it failed, he was forced to resign, as was Dulles.

Re: 8. *Bay of Pigs,* pgs. 28-29

Tracy Barnes, Senior CIA Field Officer, Project Coordinator

Barnes directed to coup against Arbenz, in Guatemala, and considered by many to be the architect of the Bay of Pigs invasion. Barnes enjoyed the complete confidence of Bissell and, as such, he was given the opportunity to choose many key personnel for the project. Among those who created a great deal of controversy, was E. Howard Hunt of Watergate "fame". In 1962, Barnes assumed the position of the CIA's Chief of Domestic Operations Division.

Jake Engler, Director of Cuban Task Force

Engler, a pseudonym, (possibly for Jacob D. Esterline), was the former CIA station chief in Caracas, Venezuela, from 1957-1960. He was assigned to the OSS in the Far East during World War II. In 1954, he was part of the operation that deposed Arbenz in Guatemala.

Author's Notes: There is enough evidence in the literature to suggest that Esterline and Engler were one-in-the-same man. For example, bother "shared" the same experiences and background with the OSS in WWII. In addition, it is not unusual for an agent, working in "shallow cover" to adopt a cover name using the same initials as their real name.

Chapter Three

That from the very instant Kennedy was briefed on the operation by Dulles; he had grave reservations about its chance of success. Never-the-less, he gave the CIA permission to finalize the plan with the understanding that under no circumstances would any US military be involved.

"If I don't know anything about it,
I'll play with it for a while then
I'll tell you what it is."

—Miles Davis

There is little doubt that the new president faced a dilemma from the very first week he was elected. He was presented with a "go" or, "no go" decision concerning the Bay of Pigs operation, an operation that he had absolutely no knowledge of prior to his election. How he resolved this political "powder keg" goes to the heart of my contention that the operation was, in fact, designed to fail. To support my theory, I first had to find the "key" that unlocked the mystery of his decision-making style which, when uncovered and understood, would reveal the here-to-fore unappreciated courage of JFK.

I begin with Sorensen's recollection of Kennedy's management style followed by a few models of decision-making including some insight about self-actualizing people (which I believe Kennedy was) and finally, I present a decision-making model that I think "fit" the President's *persona*. In *Kennedy*, (Re: 9) Sorensen tells us that the President's management style was manifested in the following ways:

— He abandoned the notion of a collective, institutionalized presidency
— He abandoned the practice of the Cabinet and National Security Council's making group decisions.
— He abolished the pyramid structure of the White House staff, all of which imposed, in his view, needless paperwork and machinery between the President and his responsible officers.
— He paid little attention to organization charts and chains of command which diluted and distributed his authority.
— He relied instead on informal meetings and direct contacts with a personal White House staff, the Budget Bureau, and *ad hoc* task forces to probe and define issues for his decisions.
— No decisions of importance were made at the Cabinet meetings and few subjects of importance were ever seriously discussed *particularly* in foreign affairs. The Cabinet, as a body, was convened largely as a symbol, to be informed, *not* consulted.
— No high-level debates, or elaborate presentations, or materials were circulated in advance.

Re: 9. *Kennedy*, pgs. 281-285

Author's Notes: All of the italics are the author's and are so noted to emphasize the President's determination to insure that he, and he alone, made all of the important decisions. This is not to say that he discounted the expertise of various Cabinet members; if a problem or issue surfaced, he would take it up with the member who had jurisdiction over the matter. The President's use of the Cabinet was in sharp contrast to Eisenhower who used it to *help* him make many decisions.

/-/-/-/-/-/-/-/-/

In Abraham Maslow's Symposium #1 (Re: 10) on values, he describes the personality characteristics of a self-actualized person: which I have paraphrased in the form of a question:

1. Did he perceive reality and accept it readily?
2. Did he behave naturally and have a need for privacy?
3. Did he show self-sufficiency as opposed to dependence?
4. Did he appreciate and enjoy life and transcend the ordinary through peak experiences?
5. Did he show brotherly love and social interest, including strong friends?
6. Did he possess a democratic, egalitarian attitude?
7. Was he able to focus directly on problems?
8. Did he express values and know the difference between right and wrong?
9. Did he have a broad philosophical sense of humor?
10. Was he inventive and creative; see things in new ways?
11. Did he resist the pressures of society to conform?
12. Was he well integrated, total, and entire?
13. Was he able to transcend differences; bring together opposites?

Re: 10. "Self-actualizing People: A Study of Psychological Health", Grune & Stratton: New York (1958)

How many of the above personality characteristics could you, the reader, associate with the President? Those of us, who are old enough to remember him, know most describe the President. For those of you who are not, he had a great sense of humor, exhibited a great love of family, was never at a loss for works, he fought for civil rights, struggled to alleviate poverty and hunger, enjoyed and appreciated sports and the arts, accepted responsibility, and had a totally integrated and entire personality.

Now that I have presented Sorensen's "take" of the President's style of management, and Maslow's personality profile of self-actualized individual, I am going to offer the reader two drastically different models of decision-making and then, "marry-up" one of the two with Sorensen and Maslow.

The Rational Model (Re: 11)

The Rational Model represents the classical approach to decision-making; it provides the foundation for the quantitative disciplines such as mathematics and economics. The model is based on "scientific" concepts articulated by Frederick W. Taylor, the "father" of Scientific Management. The basic assumption of this model (and the most fragile) is that the decision maker has all of the facts concerning alternative courses of action, can quantify them numerically and literally compute the "value" of each course. The alternative that offers the greatest value

1. Then becomes the "rational" choice of action for the decision—maker to adopt. The basic assumptions of this model are:
2. There is only one decision-maker
3. The decision-maker has only one objective (profit)
4. The potential states (or conditions) of nature and courses of action are finite and have been correctly identified.

Re: 11. *The Managerial Decision-Making Process,* by E. Frank Harrison 3d Ed., Houghton-Mifflin (1987) Boston, MA

As I indicated, the Rational Model represents the classical approach to decision-making and is the only usually prescribed and taught in business schools for decision-makers in the private sector.

The Political Model (Re: 12)

The Political Model is the preferred model for most successful decision-makers in the public sector. Because of its incremental nature, it is often referred to as "The Theory of Muddling Through"—(laughed at perhaps-but not scorned). The characteristics of this model are:

1. It has an orientation for short-term results.
2. It aims at an outcome that is acceptable to many external constituencies.
3. It calls for the decision-maker to monitor a variety of power centers operating in the field of the situation at hand.
4. Consequently, the final decision is not unique or even right; it develops with the continuous reformulation of the issues relating to the situation.
5. It is remedial, geared more to the alleviation of the ever present, concrete imperfections than to the promotion of future goals.

6. It allows for countless end-means and means-ends adjustments that, in effect, make the decision more manageable.

7. Thus, there is no one decision or "right" choice but a never-ending series of attacks on the decision at hand through individual analysis and evaluation of each aspect of the decision.

Re: 12. Ibid

The difference between the Rational Model and the Incremental or Political Model can be understood using the following illustration:

> Visualize yourself at the edge of a river. It is winter and the river is frozen over. Your objective is to walk across the river to the other side without falling through the ice. If you choose the Rational Model to decide, you will first try to determine a number of potential or alternative places to cross the river. Then you would develop some criteria for selecting the optimal crossing point. For criterion, you might consider your weight, the temperature, the width of the river at the various points of your alternative routes, the length of time that the river has been frozen, and possibly, any experience that you may have had in previous river crossings. Then, by using the some sort of numerical analysis, you would *quantify* the "one best" point to cross the river. Having done that, you would cross over the ice at that point. If you made it safely across, fine! If not, you would perhaps drown.

> If you chose the Political Model, using judgment and intuition (instead of a numerical formula), you would choose a point to cross over the ice and start out—*one step at a time!* At each step, you would test the ice before taking the next step. If the ice showed any sign of weakness, you immediately change direction either to the left or right until you found a safe route. If no safe route were found, you would simply return to the safety of the riverbank—having lost nothing and risked less! Avoiding *political risk* is the value of this model.

In summery, when you combine the President's management style and his decision-making style with his personality profile of the self-actualized individual, I believe that you, the reader, now have a clear understanding of the "why" and "wherefores" of the President's actions before, during, and after the Bay of Pigs fiasco.

Chapter Four

That immediately after assuming office in January 1961, pressure began building for him to set the operation in motion. Faced with a political dilemma of monumental proportions, the President allowed the operation to go forward after assurances from Dulles that it would be successful without any intervention of US military forces.

God created the heavens and the earth in six days
but He had the advantage working alone.

—Anon.

There is no question that, after taking office, the President was subject to tremendous pressure to take action against the Castro regime. Here is how Sorensen described it: (Re: 13) (all of the italics are mine):

"He was in effect asked if he was as willing as the Republicans to permit and assist these exiles to free their own island from dictatorship, or whether he was willing to liquidate well-laid preparations, *leave* Cuba free to *subvert* the hemisphere, disband an *impatient* army in training for nearly a year under miserable conditions, and *have them spread the word* that Kennedy had *betrayed* their attempt to depose Castro . . . Moreover, the President had been told that this plan was 'now or never' for three reasons:

First, because the brigade was *fully* trained, *restive* to fight and *difficult* to hold off.

Second, because Guatemala was under pressure to close the increasingly publicized and *politically* controversial training camps and his *only* choice was to send them back to Cuba, where they wished to go, or bring them back to this country where they would *broadcast their resentment,* and,

Third, because Russian arms would soon build up Castro's army.

According to Charles J.V. Murphy, (Re: 14) just 13 days before the date set, Bissell conducted a final review of the proposed strategy. On hand were the following:

1. Dean Rusk   : Secretary of State
2. Robert McNamara   : Secretary of Defense
3. Douglas Dillon   : Secretary of Treasury
4. General Lyman Lemnitzer   : Chairman, Joint Cheifs
5. Allen Dulles   : Director, CIA
6. McGeorge Bundy   : JFK's special assistant for national security affairs.
7. Paul Nitze   : JFK's specialist on strategic planning at the Pentagon
8. Thomas Mann   : Assistant Secretary of State for Latin American Affairs
9. Adolf Berle   : JFK's Latin American Affairs specialist
10. Arthur M. Schlesinger Jr.   : (same as Berle)

11. Richard Goodwin   : (same as Berle)
12. President Kennedy

All but one of these men were part of the Executive Branch of Government. The lone "outsider"; Senator Fulbright. All but Senator Fulbright answered to the President of the United States.

This was, in effect, *a council of war*. Bissell presented his briefing on the operation followed by Dulles who summed up the risks and the prospects. Following the briefing, Fulbright spoke up, condemning the operation as the wrong thing for the U.S. to get involved in. According to Murphy, Kennedy chose not to meet the issue. Instead, going around the room, he asked his advisors whether they thought the operations should go forward. Without exception, the answer was "yes".

In retrospect (and after-the-fact), there were those in the group who were not in favor or, were "on the fence". I might also suggest that there was at least one who didn't care one way or the other! Then, why did they all (except Fulbright), vote "yes"? I believe that there were at least three reasons: (1) they were firmly committed to the operation, (2) those on the fence voted for the operation because they did not want to frustrate the President as Senator Fulbright had apparently done, and (3) those, or that one person, who didn't care on e way or another but voted "yes" with the group.

I was not personally familiar with the men at that briefing except for one; as a young officer in Korea, in the 1950's, I did meet with General Lemnitzer, then commander of the Eighth Army. From that meeting, I came away with the opinion (along with my fellow officers) that he was a "no nonsense" soldier who would not be afraid to offer his opinion even if he *were not asked* for it. However, there were a few factors that were "unique" to his role and situation that motivated him to vote "yes" on the operation:

First, the General's boss, Robert McNamara, the Secretary of Defense, had voted "yes" to the plan. Given McNamara's tight grip on the armed services, it is highly unlikely that the General would risk a "no" vote.

Re: 13. *Kennedy* pg. 295

Re: 14. "President Kennedy, The CIA, And The Bay of Pigs", *Fortune Magazine*, 1961

Second, I seriously doubt that the removal of Castro was a high priority of the Joint Chiefs. After all, we were in the middle of the Cold War and, militarily, Castro was not a threat to U.S. security.

Third, it is not unreasonable to assume that the General was aware that "Ike", who masterminded the defeat of Hitler, had given his approval, at least in principle, to the plan (*as he understood it*).

Finally, I believe that the General and the Joint Chiefs were comfortable with the fact that it was the CIA's "baby" to win or to lose i.e.: It is more than possible that they thought of the operation as a "win-win" situation for them. If the operation was successful, it would be a win for the forces of democracy. If it failed, it could still be a "win" in that it would seriously damage the credibility of the CIA and put an end to their conduct of what can best be described as their "private wars". Consequently, I believe that the General believed that the Pentagon had everything to win and nothing to lose by approving the plan.

Author's Notes: Another reason that many members of the *war council* may have voted in favor of the operation is that they could have assumed that the planners were "holding back" some elements of the operation; intelligence that was known only to them i.e.: Some information that assured success of the operation but was too sensitive to reveal even the group. This assumption would not be unrealistic. In the intelligence "business", you are only told what the responsible intelligence agency wants you to know. Even within the agency itself, only a few key players know the *whole* plan. This is referred to as "compartmentation". This is done for two reasons. First, compartmentation assures security of the operation and secondly, it assures *control* of the operation. The operation was, as you must remember: "The CIA all the way".

/-/-/-/-/-/-/-/-/

With reference to the above, "author's notes", there was plenty that the operation planners were not telling! (But it was not good) For example:

Cuban intelligence, the DGI, had infiltrated the counter revolutionary forces not only in the U.S. but also those within Cuba. As early as July 1959, "Castro's intelligence chief, Major Ramiro Valdez, began secret meetings in Mexico City with the Soviet Ambassador and KGB residency.

The KGB dispatched over a hundred advisors to overhaul Castro's security and intelligence system, many drawn from the ranks of *los niños*, the children of Spanish Communist refugees who had settled in Russia after the Civil War. One Spanish Republican veteran, Enrique Lister Farjan, organized the Committees for the Defense of the Revolution, a Cuban neighborhood watch system to keep track of counterrevolutionary subversion. Another, General Alberto Bajar, set up a series of guerrilla training schools." (Re: 15) In addition, in 1961, Castro, with the help of the Soviet Union, had one of the largest, best trained, and best-equipped army in Central America. There was no way, by any stretch of the imagination, that the "rag-tag" invasion force could defeat Castro's Revolutionary Army! The Soviet advisors had done their job well!

Author's Notes: For those that may not know, or may not remember, the Spanish Civil War began in approximately 1936 and was fought between the Nationalists, under the leadership of General Franco and the Republican Army (those loyal to the government). Joining the Republican Army were many left-wing volunteers from several countries including the U.S. and the Soviet Union. Franco eventually won becoming Spain's Dictator. Many of the Spaniards who were lucky enough to escape the killing and imprisonment, took up residence in the Soviet Union.

Re: 15. KGB: The Inside Story, by Christopher Andrew & Oleg Gordievsky, Harper Collins Publisher (1990) pg. 467

Chapter Five

That from the very beginning, the President realized that the operation was fatally flawed and took steps to insure its failure. In the process, he avoided a confrontation with the Soviet Union.

"The importance of a decision is not how much it costs, but how quickly it can be reversed if it is wrong."

—Peter F. Drucker,
Management Consultant

Before moving on to the actual invasion, let's examine the plan a little more thoroughly (as opposed to *after* the failure). Was the operation simply a poorly planned and poorly executed or was it well planned and poorly executed? Historically, we know that it was poorly executed. Knowing that much, *the plan*, is the only remaining question; how good was it? On paper it looked good. On paper, it *should* have succeeded. But *planning is a process*; first, you identify the objective. *Next*, you develop a series of alternatives (or options); you determine critical criteria that you think will ensure the success of the plan, and *finally*, measure the criteria against each alternative. The alternative that measures the "highest" potential for success is the one chosen. If these steps are followed, then we can assume that it is a good plan; otherwise, *it is poorly planned*. Not to belabor the point, but if, for instance, the chosen plan has a weak point then *reasonable* decision-makers *must* view the plan as *flawed*. Given the intellectual resources of the planning group, on one will ever convince me that failure was not considered! Not only that, but they must have known that with failure, *comes consequences*! *Question:* Were the CIA planners too close to the plan or, so "in love" with the operation that they developed a severe case of myopia?

Author's Notes: In management, there is a term that is used to describe group members who lose their ability to think as individuals and conform to group decision-making at the expense of their good judgment. That term is "Groupthink". A group in this mode loses its ability to make logical decisions.

/-/-/-/-/-/-/-/-/

One obvious flaw in the plan dealt with the preparedness of the brigade as reported by the CIA. Recall, if you will, my conversation with "Pepe" on the condition of the brigade. He told of his training in Guatemala where conditions were "intolerable". He claimed that the troops were poorly trained and poorly equipped; that ammunition was scarce and that his battalion was undermanned. There is ample evidence to support his contention.

The bottom line is that the brigade was not prepared for combat! I learned "first-hand" the frustration and resentment of someone who actually participated in the invasion. "Pepe" also recounted that there were many acts of heroism that went unnoticed and unreported. There were no medals, no parade, no victory, only prison or death.

Another critical factor in the brigade's "readiness" was the leadership factor. The literature regarding the struggle for leadership within the brigade would fill a library. On the one hand, was the *Frente*, the Cuban government in exile who wanted to control the operation. On the other, was the CIA, *Bissell et al.* But that wasn't all! . . .

"As the brigade grew, there were now five hundred men in training—the Byzantine political complexities of Miami spilled over into the Guatemalan camps. The Americans in charge, all officers borrowed by the CIA from the armed services, became vexed, then frantic. No military operation could work unless people followed orders. The Cubans didn't bother challenging orders; they argued about who should have the right to issue orders in the first place . . . . Rodolfo Nodal* joined the debate with fervor . . . . Like all Cubans, Nodal knew that the Americans were indispensable to his cause. But, watching how the camp commander "Colonel Frank" and the U.S. command of thirty-eight 'advisors' lorded it over the Brigade from their hilltop residence 'like mandarins over a Chinese province', Nodal seethed. Control should not be in the hands of foreigners, however friendly. It should rest with the Frente and its own designated general staff in Florida . . . . Hopefully, they would not condone the recent relaxation of recruiting standards and allow Batistanos into the brigade". (Re: 16)

Author's Notes: If you recall, *Batistanos* was a name given to those exiles that had served in the ex-dictator's government.

/-/-/-/-/-/-/-/-/

In actuality, the President *had* issued an order excluding the *Batistanos* from the brigade, but unknown to the President, the CIA ignored the ban. Former Batiste officers, including the San Roman brothers, Roberto and Pepe (no relation to my contact), were given important commands because, as the CIA explained it, "they were experienced military men and, more important, proven anti-communists." (Re: 17) (In retrospect, the brothers were among those who distinguished themselves during the invasion).

---

*   Nodal, son of the former Cuban Defense Minister, now Communications Officer, 2d Battalion, Cuban Brigade.

Re: 16. *Bay of Pigs,* by Wyden, pgs. 57/58

Ignoring the President's order not to use Batistanos was not the only one issued by the President that the CIA ignored. According to Robert Kennedy, "In fact, we found out later that, despite the President's orders that no American forces would be used, the first two people who landed in the Bay of Pigs were Americans. The CIA sent them in. I think that there is a book out on the Bay of Pigs—[Endino] Oliva, [Roberto] San Roman, [Enrico] Williams, and [Manuel] Artime, the four of them—that will indicate that some officers (Americans) down in Guatemala, in Central America, had said even if the President attempted to call off the invasion . . . . that they would make arrangements with the Cubans to turn over their arms and be captured and that they should go ahead with the invasion in any case. Virtually treason!" (Re: 18)

Author's Notes: According to Wyden (pg. 160n), the two Americans who were the first ashore were "Grey" Lynch and "Rip" Robertson.

Re: 17. *CIA: The Inside Story,* by Andrew Tully, Wm Morrow & Co., NY (1962), pg. 249

Re: 18. Robert Kennedy: In His Own Words, Bantam Press (1988) pg. 240

/-/-/-/-/-/-/-/-/

Another question that begs to be asked is: Why would Kennedy, at the zenith of his political career, and Bissell, next-in-line for the top post in the CIA, risk everything on such an obviously and dangerously flawed adventure? Except for a very few at the top (including Kennedy), I believed that there was an event planned to take place at the start of the invasion that, if successful, would destabilize the entire Island and the Castro regime from top to bottom! That event would be assassination of Fidel Castro!

Of course, the thought of assassinating Castro wasn't "born" into the Bay of Pigs operation. Quite the contrary, it had been in the CIA's womb for some time *before* the Bay of Pigs. The only problem was that none of the operational plans developed by the CIA ever worked! Granted, most had been "harebrain" schemes with poison being the "weapon of choice". Apparently, there were lots of assassins *willing* to accomplish the deed but they had all gotten cold feet at the last minute. However, this time, the promoter of the idea to assassinate Castro at the moment of the invasion decided to try a "novel" approach, hire the Mafia to do it! I believe, and I cannot recall the specific reference, that mob-boss, Sam Trafficante, was initially contacted by an ex-FBI* agent, in 1960, towards the end of the Eisenhower Administration, to explore the possibility of a mob connection in Havana that would be willing to assassinate Castro. Again, as I recall, Trafficante was non-committal at the time. To be sure, he wanted to see Castro out of the picture so that the mafia could resume their operations in Cuba. The reason he stalled on the proposal was because no one could be sure who would be the next president and Sam didn't want to waste "a favor" on Nixon in the event he lost the election. When Kennedy won, it apparently changed Sam's mind. Much later, in front of the House Assassinations Committee, "Trafficante admitted to having served as interpreter at a March 1961 Miami meeting among some Cuban exiles, Vegas mobster Rosselli, and Hughes's ** aide Robert Mahue [ex-FBI agent]. The men discussed any kind of way that was possible to get rid of Castro—a cannon pills, tanks, airplanes, anything." (Re: 19)

Author's Notes: The attempt to recruit the mafia may have been part of an effort called *Operation Mongoose* which had been an on-going CIA operation long before Kennedy became president. However, after the Bay of Pigs fiasco, both the president and his brother Bobby (now Attorney General) were consumed with the idea of getting rid of Castro. Their selection to head up the effort was General Edward Lansdale, a dashing CIA operative who had made his reputation by destabilizing foreign governments. Operation Mongoose's objective was to "kill the cobra" (Castro) by any means possible. As the reader will discover, Lansdale becomes a key figure in Part II of this book.

/-/-/-/-/-/-/-/-/

As the President awaited news of the invasion, he must have also wondered if Castro was dead or alive. We know, in retrospect (always 100%), that he lived.

I know that at the beginning of this chapter, I gave the impression that I would be "moving on to the actual invasion". However, so much has already been written about it and so much is known, I don't believe that I can add anything other than some elements of the invasion that will support my contention that the operation was designed to fail. I will begin my stating

---

** That would be billionaire Howard Hughes.

"flat out" that I do not know if the planners *intended* for it to fail or not! On the other hand, it is almost impossible for me to believe that *anyone* in the agency thought it would work! From the President's point of view, I believe that he allowed the operation to go forward from the standpoint of it being a *political* expediency. To substantiate that conclusion, I offer the following evidence:

— All during the Presidential election of 1960, Kennedy had castigated the Eisenhower administration for (1) not doing anything about Cuba and (2) for not helping the Cuban exiles free their own country.
— After taking office in January 1961, he did approve the plan that the CIA developed using Cuban exiles but only on that they could carry it out without any U.S. military support.
— Instead of allowing the CIA full control of the operation, he made a critical decision on the eve of the invasion to cancel the second air strike, which was destined to support the landing of the invasion force thus, ensuring total defeat of the operation.

Recall from Chapter Four, just 13 days before the scheduled invasion, that Mr. Kennedy conducted a meeting on the Bay of Pigs Operation at which time, he had gone around the room asking for a vote of either "yes" or "no" and, without one dissenting vote, they all said "yes". My contention that the President intended for the invasion to fail is further substantiated by Mr. Murphy:

"Kennedy, either at the meeting or soon after, made two separate rulings that were to contribute to the fatal dismemberment of the whole plan. First, U.S. air power would not be called at any time. Second, the obsolescent B-26's flown by 'our' Cubans could be used in only two strikes before the invasion; first on D-minus two days (April 15) and again on the morning of the landing". (Re: 20) Sorensen's account is even more to the point: "The principal condition on which he insisted before approving the plan was to rule out any direct, overt participation of American armed forces in Cuba. Although it is not clear whether this represented any change in policy, this decision—while in one sense *permitting the disaster* which occurred—in another *helped to prevent a far greater one*". (Re: 12) (Author's italics)

The two quotes from Murphy and Sorensen are, in my opinion, sufficient *proof-positive* that the President intended from the very start, to control this operation by holding the "reigns of reason" over it. I believe that this is demonstrated by his action in canceling the second air strike. Both of these quotes substantiate my source's claim that the operations' failure was built *into it*, i.e.: It was designed to fail.

19. *The Man Who Knew Too Much,* by Dick Russell, Carroll & Graf Publishers (1992), pg. 436
20. "President Kennedy . . . " (Murphy)
21. Kennedy (Sorensen) pg. 297

Chapter Six

Epilogue

"A camel is a horse put together by a committee"

—Unknown

Again and again, the critics of my conclusions will argue that the Bay of Pigs operation was not designed to fail, and if they want to "pick fly manure out of pepper" they can make a good case that it was not ("they" of course, would be the planners). In any case, I would remind them of an old management axiom: "A brilliant plan poorly executed is no better than a poor plan brilliantly executed". You may take your pick however, the result will be the same—Failure!

Given the fact that the President had *grave* doubts about the success of the operation from the very beginning i.e.: From the time he was briefed just after he was elected in November 1960, why would a man of his intellectual capacity, agree to it in the first place? Perhaps, "Kennedy felt he was on a roll. He won the nomination and he won the election. He figured things were going his way and, he tossed the dice one more time". (Re: 22) In effect, the President engaged in a "crap-shoot" . . . and lost! Or, *did he lose?*

At this time, I would like to "play back", as it were, the comment the President-elect made (as recorded by Sorensen): "that he might call the whole thing off if he had a change of mind". I believe that that statement "opens the door" to his decision-making style. Furthermore, I believe that his decision-making style "begs" more attention to be given to the "whys and wherefores" of his actions leading up to and during the whole Bay of Pigs episode. To sustain my previous statement, I invite the reader to compare Kennedy's decisions with the Political Model of decision-making first offered in Chapter Three. A recap of the model is presented in Exhibit 6-1. I believe that a thorough analysis of each of the President's decisions regarding the Bay of Pigs can be associated with and found in conjunction with every element of the Political Model. In doing so, nearly everything the President did becomes understood and "rational".

Re: 22. The Dark Side of Camelot, by Seymour Hersh, Published by Little, Brown and Company (1997), pgs. 202/203

The Political Decision Model

1. It has an orientation for short-term results.
2. It aims at an outcome that is acceptable to many external constituencies.
3. It calls for the decision-maker to monitor a variety of power centers operating in the field of the situation at hand.
4. Consequently, the final decision is not unique or even right; it develops with the continuous reformulation of the issues relating to the situation.
5. It is remedial, geared more to the alleviation of the ever present, concrete imperfections, than to the promotion of future goals.
6. It allows for countless ends-means and means-ends adjustments that, in effect, make the decision more manageable.
7. Thus, there is no one decision, or "right" choice but a never-ending series of attacks on the decision at hand through individual analysis and evaluation of each aspect of the decision.

Exhibit 6-1

What were some of the factors that influenced the President's decision-making? First, I think that when Kennedy was elected, he immediately found himself confronted with a "run-away-train" and the longer it remained on the "track", the faster it went i.e.: It demanded his undivided attention. The dilemma for him was that the problem of Cuba that he had so roundly criticized the Eisenhower administration about, suddenly and unexpectedly became his! Beyond the campaign rhetoric just how important was the Cuban situation to him? Did the success of the operation only offer a marginal defeat for the global communism, or, would its success create a real threat to world peace? (The Soviets had threatened that an American invasion of Cuba would not go unmet!). (Re: 23) Perhaps, more important to him than Cuba was the situation in Laos, a country where fighting had broken out between communist and anti-communist forces; fighting that threatened to engulf the entire Indochina Peninsula.

Before leaving office, Eisenhower had warned Kennedy that Laos presented a major problem for the new administration. As early as 1952, the Army "Brass" had seen the need for a different approach in fighting the spread of Communism. In those days, following WWII, The "Domino Theory" i.e.: The ultimate communist domination of the world, one country at a time, was uppermost in the minds of the Free-world's military and political leaders. During this period, Red China (in the East) and the Soviet Union (in the West) were aggressively pursuing their aims; politically, if possible, militarily, if necessary. The problem for the U.S. and other western countries was how to combat this spread of communism without starting World War III. In the U.S., solving (or addressing) this problem was given to the U.S. military.* In response, the Army established the U.S. Army Special Forces, in 1952. A school for training Special Forces (SF) was established at Fort Benning, Georgia, that same year. In essence, the mission of SF was to surreptitiously enter a target country, conduct combat operations against the enemy, and get away without being detected.

In the Eisenhower Administration, one of the first target countries in which SF was deployed, was Laos. In this author's view, this action served to underscore Eisenhower's concern that Laos would be the first "domino" to fall in Southeast Asia.

23. *CIA: The Inside Story,* by Andrew Tully, William Morrow & Co. Publishers (19*62) pg. 250

Author's Notes: I had a number of personal friends who had served in Laos, in both the 50's and 60's. It was a difficult and dangerous assignment. One of my friends was a teacher who was "sent into" to teach Laotian troops how to speak English. Others were attached to Laotian units. Laotians, being very superstitious, would aim their artillery pieces straight up in the air and fire on an eclipse of the moon thinking that the sun's shadow on the moon was an evil spirit. Of course, what goes up must come down!

/-/-/-/-/-/-/-/-/

I mention all of these things about "Ike" and Laos to support my belief that, when Eisenhower "briefed" the new president, he must have emphasized the importance of "saving" Indochina from a Communist take-over. That is why I believe that Kennedy was more interested in that part of the world than he was in Cuba. Within the context of the "Political Model", the *extinction* of the Cuban problem, i.e.: Its failure, allowed him to turn his attention toward the bigger problem in Southeast Asia. In retrospect, neither Eisenhower nor Kennedy were fools. Eisenhower was not only a great general but he was also an astute politician; he allowed the CIA to develop the plan but not to carry it out in his administration. Instead, he decided to let the new president deal with it. Kennedy possessed political savvy, which was on a par with Ike's. In military strategy, he was no match for the general. He was not, however, totally devoid of military operations. After all, he was a naval hero who had served as a PT Boat Commander in the South Pacific. As such, one would have to conclude that he had some knowledge of military strategy and tactics. From the very beginning, he must have known that the Bay of Pigs was just an "adventure" doomed to failure. His decision to ensure its failure may have set in motion the events that would end in his assassination.

PART II

Investigation Into The Assassination
Of President John F. Kennedy

George H.W. Bush, Former Director of CIA and Author
(CIRCA 1999)

Preface

Are there any among us, 50 years or older, who do not remember where you were, the day and the hour, we heard the news that the President had been shot? Like you, I remember it well. At the time, I was a Special Agent, assigned to the US Army's 115th Military Intelligence Group, at Fort MacArthur, California, near San Pedro. On the morning of November 22nd, 1963, I was on my way to Long Beach State College to conduct an interview of a character reference supplied to me by an individual in the U.S. Army who was being considered for a security clearance. As I approached the campus, word came over the radio that the President had been shot! I was so shocked by the news that I pulled off the road and parked under a tree. I was not particularly fond of Kennedy; as a matter of fact, I had voted for the then Vice President Nixon. However, the President was my Commander-in-Chief and the thought that someone wanted him dead was inconceivable to me.

As I sat in my car, I commiserated over what I should do next; return to my office at Fort MacArthur, or, continue on and try to complete my task. Since I was already on campus, I decided to do the interview, and then return to my office. (The thought had occurred to me that, as a result of the shooting, the whole of the U.S. Army may have been placed on full alert) Within minutes, I was at the dormitory of my character reference. When I entered, I found everyone gathered around the television set in their lounge. I stood there for several moments, transfixed by the news and pictures of the tragic event. My assignment suddenly assumed minuscule proportions in relation to the reality of the situation. With some hesitation, I made my presence known and called out the name of the individual that I had come to see. Instantly, all eyes were focused on me. Within seconds, a young man rose from a sofa and made his way toward me. I mentioned for him to follow me into the hallway. There, I introduced myself and revealed my purpose for wanting to talk to him.

After the interview, I thanked him for his cooperation and we went our separate ways, he back to the lounge, and I, back to Fort MacArthur and my office.

Back at the office, I learned that a general alert had been issued for all of our troops overseas. In the U.S., however, only the 112th Military Intelligence Group, in Dallas, had been ordered to "stand by". Frankly, I was greatly relieved that my Group was not affected. Little did I know that within a few short months, and in a place halfway around the world, I would be thrust into the "mix" of the assassination conspiracy!

"The king is not saved by a mighty army;
A warrior is not delivered by great strength;
A horse is a false hope for victory, nor does it
deliver anyone by its great strength"

Psalm 33:16-17

Introduction

In the summer of 1964, I was transferred from my assignment at Fort MacArthur, California, to West Germany. Of course, that was before the reunification of Germany. My final destination was Schweinfurt, a small town near Wurtzburg. My unit assignment was the 3rd Military Intelligence Detachment (MID) 3rd Infantry Division. Our mission was to guard against any espionage activity directed against the division specifically, and the US Army in general.

I was well acquainted with Schweinfurt and Conn Barracks (outside of town) where my office was located. In 1951, I had been a member of Tank Company, 22nd Infantry Regiment, 4th Infantry Division, located at Conn Barracks. My old barracks was just a "stones" throw from my office. The area, rural in nature, was just as beautiful as I had remembered it. In retrospect, I had spent many days with my buddies "jockeying" big M-26 medium tanks over the roads, fields and forests of West Germany. Nearly all of the men of Tank Company were draftees as a result of the Korean War. Most were of an average age of 25 and, except for myself, were drafted out of the workforce. As for me, I was attending the College of Music in Cincinnati, Ohio, when I "was called". Most of our cadre were combat veterans having served first in Africa, then in the liberation of Western Europe. They were some of the Army's finest. Consequently, we were a "cocky", confident, combat-ready team. Yes, Conn Barracks held many fond memories for me.

During WWII, the facility had been home to the Luftwaffe. By day, German warplanes were under camouflage and sheep roamed the area. From all appearances, the area was just another peaceful rural landscape. By night, German fighter planes "scrambled" to meet Allied bomber who had made Schweinfurt a favorite target—Schweinfurt was the center of the German ball-bearing producing factories. In addition, Schweinfurt had been the town singled out by the Allied High Command for a "revenge" bombing in retaliation for the destruction of Coventry by German bombers. Now, as I wandered about the airfield, I saw that it was about the same as I had left it 13 years ago; the sheep still grazed on the lush green grass and I had the feeling that the old sheep herder who looked after them now, was the same sheep man of years gone by. The scenery hadn't changed since the time that I first saw Conn Barracks but things had certainly changed for me.

Thirteen years ago, I was "Corporal" Durr, a GI in military uniform. Since Corporal was the lowest ranking non-commissioned officer in the unit, I had to march to everyone's "drum" who out ranked me. I cleaned latrines and windows, made beds, stood inspection, and had to ask permission to go anywhere other than Conn Barracks; My entire routine was controlled by someone else. Now, I was "Mr. Durr"; I wore civilian clothes and drove civilian cars. I moved around at will doing what *I thought* I should be doing. I had earned the trust and respect that few men and women in the military could ever hope to attain—no matter what their rank! I was a man on a mission and I intended to those who had placed their trust in me that they had made the right choice! Little did I know that I would soon have the opportunity to solve the greatest mystery of the 20th Century; the assassination of John F. Kennedy!

It all began to unfold one afternoon about two months after my arrival in Schweinfurt. I was sitting in my office when I heard a knock on my door. When I opened it, I was confronted by an American soldier of Hispanic descent. I invited him in and offered him a seat next to my desk. After exchanging a few pleasantries, I asked him what I could do for him. What followed was an amazing account of his seeing and hearing an individual who claimed responsibility for the assassination of President Kennedy! What a shock! Never in my wildest imagination could I ever have conceived that I would have a conversation about our dead president with a US soldier in Germany!

The soldier began by telling me that he had a number of other soldiers, all of Hispanic descent, had been invited to attend a meeting of an organization calling themselves the "Amigo d' Espanole, the "Friends of Spain". According to my soldier's source, the purpose of the organization was to foster Hispanic customs and ideas among Spanish-speaking people throughout the world. In short, association with the "club" was not limited to American soldiers; it was open to all Hispanics in the area.

Author's Notes: It was a well-known fact that many foreigners came from the Federal Republic of Germany (FRG) i.e.: West Germany seeking work. For the most part, the Germans welcomed these individuals because there were not enough Germans to meet the labor demand. Many of these foreign workers are actually recruited by the FRG. Consequently, thousands of people migrated to the FRG from all over Europe and the Near East. From a counterintelligence perspective, this presented a "nightmare". As a result, any organization with foreign roots was of interest to us.

The soldier told me that he had accidentally found out about the club from other Hispanic soldiers in his unit. As a favor to one of his friends, my source decided to attend a meeting. The first meeting he attended was boring and he had decided not to return. However, his friend told him that, at the next meeting, a former Filipino Scout was to be the guest speaker so he returned for one more meeting. The Scout began by recounting some of his experiences fighting the Japanese in WWII. Then, he dropped a "bombshell" and told the group that he and some of his former scouts had actually assassinated President Kennedy! Stunned by his pronouncement, someone in the audience asked why. "Because" he said, "the President had cancelled their retirement pensions."

I instructed the soldier to continue attending the meetings and to collect as much information as possible about the scout. I cautioned him not to take any notes during the meetings, but to write down anything he could remember as soon as he returned to his barracks.

When I had obtained all of the information that I could, I had the soldier execute a sworn statement as to the veracity of his report. I also called his commanding officer who also verified the story. In doing so, I learned that the man had first reported the event to his CO who, in turn, sent him to me. I advised the officer that we were interested in using the soldier for possible counterintelligence activities. He agreed to cooperate with me fully. Shortly after the soldier left my office, I contacted my superiors and advised them that I had opened an investigation of the incident.

The soldier returned to my office one more time to tell me that he had learned nothing new about the group. With that report, we agreed to terminate further contact unless he came into possession of any other information relative to the group or the assassination plot. Specifically, I was hoping for names but the soldier *claimed* that he did not know names of any group member. To the best of my knowledge (and his commanding officer's) the soldier's association with the group ended. A file check at the 66th Military Intelligence Group on the "Amigo d' Espanole" came up "empty". (The 66th MI Group was headquarters for all Army Intelligence units in Europe)

Once my written report was received by my commander, it was "handed-off" to a special intelligence unit for further investigation. I never received any feedback from my report and, as a result, I can only guess that it was dismissed as "unreliable". Unfortunately, the unit that the case was given to had a poor reputation for "follow-up" and was often criticized for a lackluster performance. (Yes, we had some of those people!) As for me, I believed the soldier's story and the story that the scout told him at the meeting. I have spent years trying to make some sense of the soldier's story. Now, I believe that I have uncovered enough "evidence" to move forward with my case and that my conviction has merit. In the remainder of this book, I will present the reader with the evidence that I have compiled and let them make their own decision. For starters, I offer just some facts about the Filipino Scouts that makes the soldier's story plausible. In succeeding chapters, I will try to make the connection:

First, the Scouts were superior marksmen; they could knock the eye out of an eagle at 500 years, about the length of a city block,

Second, against the Japanese, the Scouts were used by the US Army in guerrilla operations. Many of these scouts were members of the regular US Army; others can be cast as "reserves or paramilitary scouts". This is a critical factor for the readers to remember.

Third, Filipino Scouts were the most accurate and deadly snipers in the world.

Their favorite weapon in World War II was the U.S. Army's Springfield Rifle; a single-shot, breech-loaded, .30 Cal. Weapon. In later years, the *German Mauser* became the favorite weapon of guerrilla forces *worldwide.* This is another critical factor to remember.

Fourth, If there were more than one shooter involved in the assassination (as the evidence indicates) then, the concept of what I will call the "triangulation method of targeting" becomes a critical factor. The method is taught by the military to make a "sure kill". This is a method in which two different riflemen, fire at the same target from two different angles (See diagram below). This method of killing is a sniper strategy.

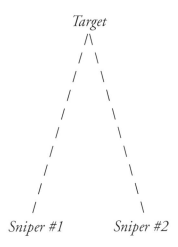

Target

Sniper #1   *Sniper #2*

Before moving on to my *List of Findings* and Chapter 1, I want to offer the reader three more factors to consider:

1. A cogent motive for the assassination has never been established "beyond a reasonable doubt". However, *if* the President *did* terminate the scouts' pension, revenge would certainly be a motive for them, at least in their eyes. But suppose he didn't, suppose someone *lead* them to believe that he had?
2. Assuming that they were *given* a motive, it would be no problem for them to get in or out of the country. They would also have had free access to move about the country without causing suspicion, especially in Texas, which has a large Hispanic population.
3. *Finally, why would anyone claim to have shot the President if they had not actually done it?*

Author's Notes: Did the President actually terminate Army benefits for this particular group of scouts? If they were told that he did, who would have been able to convince them that he had, when in fact, he had not? Obviously, it would be someone who had their *compete* faith. As far as the scout bragging about killing Kennedy (if he hadn't), wouldn't it have made more sense if he bragged about the number of Japanese he and his group had killed?

Another possibility that must be considered is that, after WWII, these para-military Filipino Scouts *never* received the full Army benefit that the "regulars" did. In *this* case, suppose that they were told that Kennedy *denied* their claim? After the war, this classification of scouts did receive some compensation for their service but not the full benefits that the regulars received. (See following Attachment). In conclusion, if these scouts actually carried out the assassination, they *would* have had *access*, their *motive* could have been cogent, and they would *definitely* had the capability; three elements needed to prove intent. I can accept the fact that they did kill President Kennedy but I know that they could not have acted alone.

To find out the "*who*" and "*why*" forms the basis of my quest. Travel with me as I explore some of the clandestine activities conducted behind closed doors and *in the shadow of the Sphinx.*

—The Author

Bill Summary & Status for the 108th Congress

Item 6 of 17

PREVIOUS | NEXT
PREVIOUS:SUMMARY | NEXT:SUMMARY
NEW SEARCH | HOME | HELP | ABOUT SUMMARIES

H.R.677
Title: To amend title 38, United States Code, to deem certain service in the organized military forces of the Government of the Commonwealth of the Philippines and the Philippine **Scouts** to have been active service for purposes of benefits under programs administered by the Secretary of Veterans Affairs.
Sponsor: Rep Cunningham, Randy (Duke) [CA-50] (introduced 2/11/2003)   **Cosponsors:** 49
Latest Major Action: 3/12/2003 Referred to House subcommittee. Status: Referred to the Subcommittee on Benefits.

SUMMARY AS OF:
2/11/2003--Introduced.

Filipino Veterans Equity Act of 2003 - Deems certain service performed before July 1, 1946, in the organized military forces of the Philippines and the Philippine **Scouts** as active military service for purposes of eligibility for veterans' benefits through the Department of Veterans Affairs. Repeals certain provisions discounting such service as qualifying service.

Author's Notes: Please read carefully the language within the above bracket.

Attachment #1 to Introduction   Page 1 of 3

GPO's PDF Display	Congressional Record References	Bill Summary & Status	Printer Friendly Display · 3,411 bytes.[Help]

Filipino Veterans Equity Act of 2003 (Introduced in House)

HR 677 IH

108th CONGRESS

1st Session

H. R. 677

To amend title 38, United States Code, to deem certain service in the organized military forces of the Government of the Commonwealth of the Philippines and the Philippine Scouts to have been active service for purposes of benefits under programs administered by the Secretary of Veterans Affairs.

IN THE HOUSE OF REPRESENTATIVES

February 11, 2003

Mr. CUNNINGHAM (for himself, Mr. FILNER, Mr. EVANS, Mr. ISSA, Ms. MILLENDER-MCDONALD, Mr. GUTIERREZ, Mr. WYNN, Mr. ABERCROMBIE, Ms. PELOSI, Mr. CASE, Ms. HARMAN, Ms. BORDALLO, Ms. LEE, Mr. ROHRABACHER, Ms. SCHAKOWSKY, Mr. ROYCE, Mr. BECERRA, Mr. INSLEE, Mr. SCOTT of Virginia, Ms. ROYBAL-ALLARD, Ms. CORRINE BROWN of Florida, Mr. FROST, Mr. DAVIS of Illinois, Mr. MCDERMOTT, Ms. LOFGREN, and Mr. LANTOS) introduced the following bill; which was referred to the Committee on Veterans' Affairs

A BILL

To amend title 38, United States Code, to deem certain service in the organized military forces of the Government of the Commonwealth of the Philippines and the Philippine Scouts to have been active service for purposes of benefits under programs administered by the Secretary of Veterans Affairs.

Be it enacted by the Senate and House of Representatives of the United States of America in Congress assembled,

SECTION 1. SHORT TITLE.

This Act may be cited as the `Filipino Veterans Equity Act of 2003`.

SEC. 2. CERTAIN SERVICE IN THE ORGANIZED MILITARY FORCES OF THE PHILIPPINES AND THE PHILIPPINE SCOUTS DEEMED TO BE ACTIVE SERVICE.

(a) IN GENERAL- Section 107 of title 38, United States Code, is amended--

(1) in subsection (a)--

(A) by striking `not` after `Army of the United States, shall`; and

(B) by striking `, except benefits under--` and all that follows in that subsection and inserting a period;

(2) in subsection (b)--

(A) by striking `not` after `Armed Forces Voluntary Recruitment Act of 1945 shall`; and

(B) by striking `except--` and all that follows in that subsection and inserting a period; and

(3) by striking subsections (c) and (d).

(b) CONFORMING AMENDMENTS- (1) The heading of such section is amended to read as follows:

`Sec. 107. Certain service deemed to be active service: service in organized military forces of the Philippines and in the Philippine Scouts`.

(2) The item relating to such section in the table of sections at the beginning of chapter 1 of such title is amended to read as follows:

`107. Certain service deemed to be active service: service in organized military forces of the Philippines and in the Philippine Scouts.`.

SEC. 3. EFFECTIVE DATE.

(a) IN GENERAL- The amendments made by this Act shall take effect on January 1, 2004.

(b) APPLICABILITY- No benefits shall accrue to any person for any period before the effective date of this Act by reason of the amendments made by this Act.

List of Findings In The Case of The Assassination of JFK

1. That the U.S. Government, concerned that there would be a Communist takeover in Southeast Asia, attempted to install a democratic form of government in South Vietnam. Through devious means, the CIA selected Ngo Dinh Diem as South Vietnam's first "democratically" elected president.
2. That a motive for the assassination of President Kennedy was in retaliation for the assassination of President Ngo Dinh Diem.
3. That other forces were at work inside South Vietnam clamoring for the removal of Diem.
4. That a motive for the assassination of Kennedy can be associated with the failure of the Bay of Pigs Operation.
5. That a motive for the assassination of Kennedy could have been his intention to withdraw all troops from Vietnam after his reelection in 1964.
6. That the assassins of the President needed a "dupe" to blame for the killing. That dupe was Oswald.
7. That the author's "person of interest" is one who had motive, access, and the resources to assassinate the President.

Chapter One

That the US Government, concerned that there would be a Communist takeover in Southeast Asia, attempted to install a Democratic form of government in South Vietnam. Through devious means, the CIA installed Ngo Dinh Diem as South Vietnam's first "democratically" elected President.

Lives of great men all remind us
We can make our lives sublime,
And, departing, leave behind us
Footprints in the sands of time.

—Longfellow

Ngo Dinh Diem, President of South Vietnam, was assassinated on November 1, 1963.* President Kennedy was assassinated on November 22, 1963, just 21 days later! Does anyone find this fact as disturbing as I do? Other than this *coincidence* (which immediately caught my eye), I had no substantive reason to believe that there was any connection between the two killings until I read a book by Marguerite Higgins; *Our Vietnam Nightmare*. In preparation, Ms Higgins, a foreign correspondent in South Vietnam for *National Geographic Magazine*, had almost unlimited access to Diem to conduct probably the most in depth interview on record. In short, her book opened my mind to the possibility Kennedy's assassination was a revenge killing stemming from the controversy that raged within the Kennedy Administration between the "Diem must go" and the "Diem must stay" proponents.

Just who was Ngo Dinh Diem? Diem was born in 1901, in the village of Phu Cam, near the City of Hue, in the Tonkin Province. He excelled as a student in a Catholic school in Hue and later, attended a French college in Hanoi where he studied for a career in civil service. As a civil servant, he quickly rose through the ranks to become Minister of Interior in 1933, (Vietnam was under the colonial rule of France). He resigned after a few months because the French were unwilling to grant the Vietnamese more freedom. Later, during WWII, he refused the Japanese Occupation Army's offer to serve in their government and, still later, after the war, due to his ardent stand against communism, he refused an offer from Ho Chi Minh to join his government.

In 1950, Diem left Vietnam for exile in the United States where he sought refuge in the Maryknoll Seminary, in New Jersey. Among his other activities at the Seminary, *he washed dishes*. (See Exhibit 1-1) In 1953, "Francis Cardinal Spellman of New York, arranged for a luncheon visit to the U.S. Supreme Court Building and introduced Ngo Dinh Diem to Justice William O. Douglas, *Senator John F. Kennedy*, Senator Mike Mansfield, Mr. Newton of the American Friends Service Committee, Mr. Costello of the Columbia Broadcasting System, and, Edmund and Gene Gregory of the Department of State. There Ngo Dinh Diem discussed Indochina for about an hour and answered questions, chiefly from Douglas and Kennedy.

Diem had been introduced to this distinguished group as a Catholic Vietnamese Nationalist." (Re: 24)

Whatever was discussed did not dissuade Diem from leaving the United States later that year and going to Belgium where he continued his exile in a Benedictine Monastery until 1954. In 1954, the Emperor Bao Dai, now in exile himself on the French Riviera, was persuaded to name Diem as Premier of his government. Diem arrived in Saigon in late June, 1954, and a few days later, was introduced to the American, Edward G. Lansdale, a shaker and mover in the Central Intelligence Agency.

Author's Notes: According to the terms of the Geneva Agreement of 1954, Vietnam was divided at the 17th Parallel i.e.: Into two countries, North and South Vietnam. (See Figure 1-1)

In October, 1954, Ngo Dinh Diem was named President of South Vietnam. The task of organizing the country for him was given to the Saigon Military Mission (SMM) headed up by "General" Lansdale and financed by the CIA (with a blank check). To say that South Vietnam was a politically fragmented country would be a gross understatement of fact. Lansdale and the SMM had their work cut out for them. Before I offer a closer look at the mission of the SMM, I want to review the U.S. actions prior to the introduction of the SMM into Vietnam. The *first* U.S. forces to be sent to Vietnam was in 1950, when the Military Assistance and Advisory Group was dispatched to the area to evaluate what, if any, assistance we could, or should, offer the French in an effort to combat Ho Chi Minh National Liberation Army (also known as the Vietminh) which was dedicated to create a unified Vietnam under the leadership of Ho—who was, by that time, a confirmed Communist. Initially, the Military Assistance and Advisory Group (MAAG) was identified as MAAG, Indochina.

Re: 24. JFK, The CIA, Vietnam . . . . by L. Fletcher Prouty, pg. 54

Figure 1-1

In 1955, it was redesignated MAAG, Vietnam. This action was the first to introduce *uniformed* US military personnel into the "mix". The mix being MAAG, Vietnam, and the SMM under the command of Lansdale. The question of whether or not Lansdale was really a military man or simply "cloaked" as one to allow him easy access into the MAAG organization remains a mystery. What is known is that he was under the control of the CIA. Now, more about the SMM:

So, what was the mission of the SMM? It is the same mission the CIA employs worldwide; to destabilize governments whose interests are considered inimical to the interests of the United States. It was the same mission that Lansdale utilized so well in the Philippines to defeat the HUK insurgency and install Ramon Magsaysay as President of the Philippines. What is the *modus operandi* of units like the SMM? "They move unobtrusively with a small team, plenty of money, and a boundless supply of equipment as backup. They make contact with the indigenous group they intend to support, regardless of who runs the government. Then they increase the level of activity until a conflict ensues. Because the CIA is not equipped or sufficiently experienced to handle such an operation when combat intensifies to that level, the military generally is called upon for support. At that time, the level of military support has risen to such an extent that this action can no longer be termed either covert or truly deniable. At that point, as in Vietnam, operational control is transferred in the best way possible, and the hostilities continue until both sides weary of the cost in men, money, material, and noncombatant lives and property." (Re: 25)

What I have done is cite Prouty's description of how these units operate—not because I did not know but because his words bear credence over mine (however, the italics are mine). It is critical to note how we got so involved in Vietnam and how the strategy bears resemblance to what the CIA *expected to happen* in the Bay of Pigs operation *but didn't!*

Recall, that the MAAG personnel were sent to Vietnam to evaluate what, if any, assistance we could, or should offer the French in an effort to combat Ho's National Liberation Army. On the other hand, the SMM was sent to Vietnam *not* to help the French but the Vietnamese. Prouty calls the SMM nothing more than "super terrorists"! "They saw their role as promoting sabotage,

Re: 25 Ibid . . . . pg. 40

subversion, labor strikes, armed uprisings, and guerilla warfare . . . The interesting aspect of the SMM was that its leaders were firm believers in the *Little Red Book* teachings of Mao Tse-tung and spread the word accordingly." (Re: 26) Keep in mind that the SMM was under the control of the CIA, *not MAAG*. Their ultimate aim was to make sue that their man, Ngo Dinh Diem, would be installed as President of South Vietnam. We know that they were successful; under the leadership of Lansdale, the SMM/CIA accomplished one of the most amazing coups in recorded history.

First of all, *they had to create a government*. In the south of Vietnam i.e.: Below the 17th parallel, there was no government structure; there were, what I would call, tribal nations *overseen* by the Emperor Bao Dai and the French Colonial Government. As far as South Vietnam was concerned, there were three powerful tribes; the Cao Dai, the Hao Hao, and the Binh Xuyen (also known as the bandits). In today's world, we might refer to the Binh Xuyen as the "Vietnamese Mafia"; they controlled all of the vice in Saigon and the surrounding areas including the gambling casinos. Since they were firmly entrenched in Saigon, they had to present the greatest challenge. In order to give Diem an army to protect him, the SMM "bought out" their leader, Le Van Vien, and "exiled" him to the South of France. They then installed his followers in to what was to become the nucleus of the Armed Forces of the Republic of South Vietnam i.e.: The ARVN! The Cai Dai and the Hao Hao were religious sects—*with an army*. Their leaders were also bought out and were "retired" to the French Riviera. Their armies who had fought each other for centuries, were now *one army?*

It is no wonder why the combat record of the ARVN was so miserable! Never the less, South Vietnam now had an army.

The next obstacle that the SMM had to overcome was how to present their man, Diem, as the logical choice "of the people" to govern the new state. In effect, Lansdale and the SMM launched a program in South Vietnam designed to win the "hearts and minds" of its basically rural population. They accomplished this by performing acts of kindness; building schools, hutches, helping with the harvesting of rice, and the giving of money; all to help the villagers. At the same time, they were promoting the election of the man who had provided all of these wonderful deeds—Diem. To the simple nature of

Re: 26 Ibid . . . , pg. 60

the people of the villages (who didn't know or even care about politics), it only made sense to elect the one responsible for all of the help that they were getting. When their man, Diem, called for a national referendum in 1955, to determine if the country was to remain an Imperial country under the emperor Bao Dai, or to become a Republic, Lansdale and the SMM was able to "swing" a 90%—plus majority for Diem thereby ensuring his election. (Of course, it helps when your people count the votes!).

Author's Notes: By this time, the reader should be getting some idea of just how much power and influence Lansdale had. In effect, he had *carte blanche* authority from Allen Dulles, Director, CIA and Allen's brother, John Foster Dulles, to do whatever was necessary to establish a nation below the 17th Parallel—which he did! Not only did he have money but he also had access to ships and aircraft to help transport as many as a million refugees (mostly Catholic) from North of the 17th Parallel to the South. He did not do it alone; in addition to the SMM, Lansdale enlisted thousands of his old Philippino buddies (and this is critical to remember), many of who were Philippino Scouts! Lansdale's exploits were "stuff" movies were made of—and they were! Probably the most famous was "*The Ugly American,* starring John Wayne, circa 1960's, (Warner Brothers?)

MARYKNOLL FATHERS AND BROTHERS

Legal Title: Catholic Foreign Mission Society of America, Inc.

Mission Promotion Department

May 10, 2001

Dr. Frank R. Durr
7337 Brookview Circle
Tampa, FL 33634-2925

Dear Doctor Durr,

Greetings and best wishes from Maryknoll.

In reply to your letter dated April 26, 2001, I have forwarded a copy to our Archives for assistance in this matter. As soon as we receive any information, we will send it to you. I sincerely pray that you are successful in your future endeavors.

Through the loyal support of our friends, Maryknoll continues to bring the Good News to God's people in need around the world. It is important that they know they have a loving Father who is faithful to His people. In the book of Isaiah, the word of God is written: "I will never forget you; I have written your name on the palms of my hands."

As surely as He doesn't forget them, He will not forget your spirit of caring concern. Neither will we, Doctor Durr, as we include you and your intentions in our Masses and prayers. All mothers are especially remembered this month.

Sincerely yours in Christ,

Father Leo Shea

Rev. Leo B. Shea, MM
Director

Exhibit 1-1

MARYKNOLL MISSION ARCHIVES

P. O. Box 305 • Maryknoll, NY 10545-0305
TEL. (914) 941-7590 Ext. 2500 • FAX (914) 941-5753
E-mail: archives@maryknoll.org • WebSite: www.maryknoll.org

June 5, 2001

Dr. Frank R. Durr, Sr.
7337 Brookview Circle
Tampa, Florida 33634-2925

Dear Dr. Durr:

Thank you for your inquiry to the Maryknoll Mission Archives regarding the late President Ngo Dinh Diem of South Vietnam.

It is correct that Mr. Diem was in residence at Maryknoll seminaries in the early 1950s, but our files contain very little information regarding his presence or activities during that time period. Mr. Diem was in residence at the Maryknoll Junior College located in Lakewood, New Jersey from late in of 1950 until the summer of 1951. He lived at the Major Seminary, located at Maryknoll, New York, until early 1954. Presumably he was in the United States to study English, though we have no record this.

Mr. Diem obviously had fond memories of Maryknoll for he did make a visit to Maryknoll in May of 1957, after he became President. I have made copies for you of the letter of invitation from Father John Comber (Superior General of Maryknoll 1956 until 1966), the response from the Vietnamese Embassy in Washington, the protocol papers sent by the State Department, and the a press release after the visit.

With respect to the origin of Mr. Diem's connection with Maryknoll, this seems to have been the result of a casual acquaintance between Bishop Raymond Lane (Superior General of Maryknoll 1946-1956) and Bishop Ngo Dinh Thuc (Vicar Apostolic of Vinh-Long Vietnam). Bishop Ngo Dinh Thuc is, as you know, President Diem's brother

Thank you again for your inquiry to the Maryknoll Mission Archives regarding the late President Ngo Dinh Diem of Vietnam. I wish you the best in your research.

Sincerely,

Brother Kevin Dargan, MM

(Exhibit 1-1)

Assistant Director Curator of the Society Collection
email: kdargan@maryknoll.org

cc Father Leo Shea MM

The Maryknoll Mission Archives is the official records repository of the Catholic Foreign Mission Society of America, Inc. (Maryknoll Fathers and Brothers) and the Maryknoll Sisters of St. Dominic, Inc. (Maryknoll Sisters)

April 17, 1957

Mr. Tran Van Chuong
2251 R Street N.W.
Washington 8, D.C.

Your Excellency,

We have read in the papers that
the President of Vietnam will be visiting the United
States during May.

His Excellency lived with us here at
Maryknoll sometime during his former stay in this
country. We would be very pleased if Mr. Ngo dinh Diem
would visit us again here at Maryknoll, New York during
his stay in this country.

We know that His Excellency will have
a very busy schedule but would be pleased if you would
extend to him on our behalf an invitation to visit
Maryknoll.

Sincerely in Christ,

Very Rev. John W. Comber, M.M.
Superior General

JWC/P

April 29, 1957

Very Rev. John W. Comber, M.M.
Maryknoll
New York

Reverend and dear Father:

I thank you very much for your kind invitation
of April 17, and I am very pleased to confirm my
telephone conversation with you.

From the very start, and even before receiving
your invitation, President Ngo Dinh Diem expressed
the desire of visiting you and Ossining and Lakewood.
It has been very difficult, however, to work out a
satisfactory schedule and I am very pleased to let you
know that President Ngo Dinh Diem and his party will
arrive at Ossining on Sunday, May 12th, at 4 p.m. for
a visit of 45 minutes.

President Ngo has expressed a desire to meet
Father Thomas O'Melia, if possible.

Sincerely yours,

Tran van Chuong
Ambassador of Viet Nam
to the United States

DEPARTMENT OF STATE
Washington, D.C.

OFFICE OF THE CHIEF OF PROTOCOL

FINAL

Members of the Vietnamese Official Party:

His Excellency Ngo Dinh Diem
President of the Republic of Viet-Nam

His Excellency Tran Van Chuong
Ambassador of Viet-Nam to the United States

Madame Chuong
(Washington and New York only)

His Excellency Nguyen Huu Chau
Secretary of State for Interior
and to the Presidency

His Excellency Tran Le Quang
Secretary of State for Public
Works and Communications

General Tran Van Don
Chief of Staff of General Staff,
Acting Senior Aide-de-Camp

Mr. Huynh Van Diem
Director General of Planning

Mr. Vu Van Thai
Administrator General of Foreign Aid

Mr. Vo Van Hai
President's Chief Private Secretary
and Acting Protocol Officer

Mr. Ton That Thien
Chief of President's Press and Information
Service, and Interpreter

Member of the Vietnamese Embassy Staff, Washington

Mr. Nguyen qui Anh
First Secretary, Embassy of Viet-Nam
(New York only)

Members of the Vietnamese Unofficial Party

Mr. Nguyen Dinh Gia
President's Personal Staff

Mr. Tran Van An
President's Personal Staff

(continued)

Members of the American Official Party:

The Honorable Wiley T. Buchanan, Jr.,
    Chief of Protocol

Mrs. Buchanan
(Washington and New York only)

The Honorable Elbridge Durbrow,
    American Ambassador to Viet-Nam

Rear Admiral D. L. Mac Donald, U.S.N.,
    American Aide to the President of the Republic of Viet-Nam
(Washington only)

Mr. Victor Purse
    Deputy Chief of Protocol

Mr. Stuart P. Lillico
    Press Officer, Department of State

Members of the American Unofficial Party:

Mr. Frank Madden
    Security Officer, Department of State

Mr. Joseph Rosetti
    Security Officer, Department of State

(continued)

DEPARTMENT OF STATE
Washington, D.C.

OFFICE OF THE CHIEF OF PROTOCOL

STATE VISIT OF THE PRESIDENT OF THE REPUBLIC OF VIET-NAM TO THE UNITED STATES
May 1957
List of Members of the Official and Unofficial Parties

Members of the Vietnamese Official Party:

[His Excellency Ngo Dinh Diem]   (Speaks some English)
   President of the Republic of Viet-Nam
       * The President of the Republic of Viet-Nam
       ** Mr. President, Excellency, or Sir

Pronounced: NNHO DEAN DEE-YEM
   Ngo   N-O   as in "no" with a nasal "N" NNHO
   Dinh   Dinh rhymes with Dean   DEAN
   Diem   Dee-yem   DEE-YEM

His Excellency Tran Van Chuong   (Speaks excellent English)
   Ambassador of Viet-Nam to the United States
       * The Ambassador of Viet-Nam
       ** Mr. Ambassador

Pronounced: TRAN VAN CHEW-UNG
   Tran   Tran rhymes with ran TRAN
   Van   Van   rhymes with ran VAN
   Chuong Chew-ung   CHEW-UNG

Madame Tran Van Chuong (Washington and New York only) (Speaks fair English)

His Excellency Nguyen Huu Chau   (Does not speak English)
   Secretary of State for Interior
     and to the Presidency
       * His Excellency Nguyen Huu Chau
       ** Mr. Secretary

Pronounced: NHEW-YEN WHO CHOW
   Nguyen N-ew with a nasal "N" NHEW-YEN
   Huu   who   WHO
   Chau   chow   CHOW

His Excellency Tran Le Quang   (Does not speak English)
   Secretary of State for Public
     Works and Communications
       * His Excellency Tran Le Quang
       ** Mr. Secretary

Pronounced: TRAN LAY KWANG
   Tran   Tran rhymes with ran TRAN
   Le   Le   rhymes with lay LAY
   Quang   Kwang rhymes with gong KWANG

* Place Card
** Address in Conversation

                                            (continued)

Members of the Vietnamese Official Party: (Continued)

General Tran Van Don   (Speaks fair English)
    Chief of Staff of General Staff,
    Acting Senior Aide-de-Camp
      * General Tran Van Don
      ** General Don

Pronounced: TRAN VAN DÔNE
Tran	Tran	rhymes with ran	TRAN
Van	Van	rhymes with ran	VAN
Don	Don	rhymes with cone	DÔN

Mr. Huynh Van Diem   (Does not speak English)
    Director General of Planning
      * Mr. Huynh Van Diem
      ** Mr. Diem

Pronounced: WHEEN VAN DEE-YEM
Huynh	Wheen	rhymes with queen	WHEEN
Van	Van	rhymes with ran	VAN
Diem	Dee-yem		DEE-YEM

Mr. Vu Van Thai
    Administrator General of Foreign Aid   (Speaks English well)
      * Mr. Vu Van Thai
      ** Mr. Thai

Pronounced: YOU VAN TIE
Vu	Vu	rhymes with you	YOU
Van	Van	rhymes with ran	VAN
Thai	Thai	rhymes with tie	TIE

Mr. Vo Van Hai   (Speaks fair English)
    President's Chief Private Secretary
    and Acting Protocol Officer
      * Mr. Vo Van Hai
      ** Mr. Hai

Pronounced: VO VAN HIGH
Vo	Vo	rhymes with go	VO
Van	Van	rhymes with ran	VAN
Hai	Hai	rhymes with high	HIGH

Mr. Ton That Thien   (Speaks excellent English)
    Chief of President's Press and Information
    Service, and Interpreter
      * Mr. Ton That Thien
      ** Mr. Thien

Pronounced: TONE TOT TEE-YEN
Ton	Ton	rhymes with tone	TONE
That	That	rhymes with tot	TOT
Thein	Tee-yen		TEE-YEN

* Place Card
** Address in Conversation

(continued)

Members of the Vietnamese Unofficial Party:

> Mr. Nguyen Dinh Gia
> President's Personal Staff

> Mr. Tran Van An
> President's Personal Staff

Members of the American Official Party:

> The Honorable Wiley T. Buchanan, Jr.
> Chief of Protocol
>> * Mr. Buchanan or Chief of Protocol
>> ** Ambassador Buchanan or Mr. Buchanan

> The Honorable Elbridge Durbrow
> American Ambassador to Viet-Nam
>> * Ambassador Durbrow or American Ambassador to Viet-Nam
>> ** Ambassador Durbrow or Mr. Ambassador

> Rear Admiral D. L. MacDonald (Washington only)
> American Aide to the President of the Republic of Viet-Nam
>> * – ** Admiral MacDonald

> Mr. Victor Purse
> Deputy Chief of Protocol
>> * – ** Mr. Purse

> Mr. Stuart P. Lillico
> Press Officer, Department of State
>> * – ** Mr. Lillico

Members of the American Unofficial Party:

> Mr. Frank Madden
> Security Officer, Department of State

> Mr. Joseph Rosetti
> Security Officer, Department of State

* Place Card
** Address in Conversation

DEPARTMENT OF STATE
Washington, D.C.

OFFICE OF THE CHIEF OF PROTOCOL

Miscellaneous Information for Use During the Visit to the United States of
His Excellency Ngo Dinh Diem, President of the Republic of Viet-Nam

Correct Title: His Excellency the President of the Republic of
                                        Viet-Nam

Correct Form of
Address in Conversation: Mr. President, Excellency, or Sir

Correspondence
Salutation: Excellency: (Formal)
                                        Dear Mr. President: (Informal)

Correspondence
Complimentary Close: Very respectfully, (Formal general usage)
                                        Sincerely yours, (Informal)

Envelope Address: His Excellency
                                            Ngo Dinh Diem,
                                                President of the Republic of Viet-Nam,
                                                Local Address.

"In honor of" line on   In honor of His Excellency the President of the
  Invitations: Republic of Viet-Nam

Place Cards: The President of the Republic of Viet-Nam

Flags: When the flags of the United States and Viet-Nam
                                        are used, consider the area where the flags are
                                        to be placed as a stage or a focal point, then
                                        place the flag of the United States on the left
                                        as viewed from the audience, and the flag of
                                        Viet-Nam on the right.

                                        The national flag of the Republic of Viet-Nam
                                        is made up of three horizontal red stripes on
                                        a golden yellow ground. The three stripes are
                                        equal in width and equidistant from each other.
                                        Together with the spaces between them they make
                                        up the horizontal middle third of the flag.
                                        The three stripes represent the three traditional
                                        regions of Viet-Nam, north, center and south.
                                        Yellow and red are the traditional colors of
                                        Viet-Nam and possess a high mystical value for
                                        the Vietnamese people. Yellow, the imperial
                                        color is the symbol of independence. Red is a
                                        lucky color, the symbol of success.

                                                            (continued)

- 1 -

Toasts: First toast should always be made by the host "To the President of the Republic of Viet-Nam". Response will be made in a toast to the President of the United States. (Subsequent toasts, if any, may be made to other persons in declining importance).

Pronunciation: NGO: N-Ō as in "no" with a nasal "N" ("NNHO")

DINH: DEAN

DIEM: DEE - YEM

NNHO DEAN DEE-YEM

National Anthems: Except at outdoor functions where there may be honor troops and military bands, it is not recommended that the national anthems of the United States and Viet-Nam be played unless the sponsoring organization is confident that the orchestra is able to play the anthems in the best manner possible. It is believed that it is much better to dispense with the national anthems than to have them poorly played. It is not necessary to play the anthems of both countries at strictly social functions or at formal luncheons and dinners as many times it creates awkward situations and inconveniences. It is not the custom in Washington to play national anthems at State dinners. When the anthems are played, it is customary to play the anthem of the visitor's country first and the anthem of the United States second.

V.P. Thursday May 16, 1957 (Evening) Number 500 - Page **III**

PRESIDENT NGO DINH DIEM'S MARYKNOLL VISIT

<u>New York</u> - May 13 (VP)

Before going to Seton Hall University where he received an honorary degree of Law, President Ngo Dinh Diem paid a visit to Maryknoll Seminary, near Ossining, New York.

At Maryknoll, the headquarters on the Catholic Foreign Mission Society of America, President Ngo Dinh Diem met a number of priests and students whom he knew when he stayed at Maryknoll during his stay in the United State in 1951-53.

At a benediction ceremony for the President, Superior General Father John Comber noted that while President Ngo Dinh Diem came to the United States to see President Eisenhower, "he came to Maryknoll to visit his friends."

Father Comber said "the entire world recognizes you a stalwart defender of Democracy" and said that in the many struggles ahead, those at Maryknoll are confident he will succeed.

"There is no compromise between truth and falsehood, just as there is no compromise between communism and democracy," Father Comber said.

In his reply, the Vietnamese leader said he was deeply moved to find himself once again at Maryknoll. He said that during his earlier stay in Maryknoll and also at the Seminary at Lakewood, New Jersey, he was able to formulate his plans for the advancement of his country.

H.

. . . .

PRESIDENT NGO DINH DIEM'S MARYKNOLL VISIT (2)

"In this house,"President Ngo-Dinh-Diem said,"I brought
into clear vision the principle I would use for the freedom of our
country . It is here that I profited so much from the guidance and counsel. It is likewise here that I made so many
contacts with Americans which helped so much."

He concluded by asking / God's blessing on the United
States for its leadership, and upon Maryknoll for its
thoughtfulness and kindness toward him and his people.

Conducting the benediction ceremony at Maryknoll
was Vicar General Rev. Father James V. Tardy. Greeting
President Ngo Dinh Diem at the gate of Maryknoll was Robert
Lefebvre, who was his tutor when President Ngo Dinh Diem
was in Maryknoll.

Following the benediction ceremony President
Ngo Dinh Diem strolled through the grounds and talked with
old friends. He expressed a desire to see his old room at
Maryknoll and unerringly led his hosts to his old room.

NEW CAODAIST POPE PAYS VISIT TO TAY NINH
PROVINCE CHIEF

Tay-Ninh (VP) - May 16

New Caodaist Pope "Thuong Sanh" Cao-Hoai-Sang,
accompanied by   Caodaist dignitaries, called on the
Chief of Tay-Ninh province on May 14.

The talks lasted about one hour. (N)

H.

Chapter Two

That a motive for the assassination of President Kennedy was in retaliation for the assassination of President Ngo Dinh Diem.

With the establishment of a government within South Vietnam and the installation of Diem as its president by the SMM, it was hoped by both Department of State and the CIA that Diem would be able to unite the diverse religions and ethnics groups within the region. I think that in the beginning, things did look promising for the new nation. From the beginning of the new nation in 1954 "at least a million refugees from Communist North Vietnam had been settled, the bureaucratic machine rescued from anarchy, and the army brought under civilian control, rebuilt, and modernized. By 1959, Free Vietnam had the *highest per-capita income in that part of Asia.*" (Re: 27) Unfortunately, a problematic situation existed with the million or so refugees; by most accounts, they were all Catholics! Where does one put one million Catholics in such a small nation as South Vietnam (with a predominantly Buddhists population)? Diem had a plan! He declared that any unused land i.e.: any land that was not under production, to be the property of the government. In this way, he was able to supply the land needs of the new population. This "seizing" of land by Diem also created dissension in the country. Add to this already volatile situation *within* the country, the Strategic Hamlet Program that created an *ideological* conflict *outside* the country.

The idea of the Strategic Hamlet Program (SHP) was first conceived and brought to Deim's attention by a British civil servant who was assigned to the British Advisory Mission in Saigon, R.G.K. Thompson. In Thompson's view, under the SHP, "An area would be cleared of opposition—that is, "pacified"—and then, as the SHP held safety, then the natives would be allowed to return to their normal ways. The object of the SHP, as he proposed it, was to protect the villagers." (Re: 28) As Prouty points out, this was a plan to pacify, or *bring peace*, to the Mekong Delta region. One of the disturbing aspects of the SHP, if not the most, is that it required the relocation of those villagers who resided "outside" of the established hamlet zone. This was another cause of resentment.

Another problem that developed over the implementation of the SHP was in the interpretation of the word "pacify". To Diem, it meant to bring "calm" to the area whereas, it (apparently) meant something totally different to U.S. Forces; "it meant to hit an area as hard as possible in order that it would be

Re: 27 *Our Vietnam Nightmare . . .* pg. 13

Re: 28 *JFK, The CIA, Vietnam . . .* pg. 251

reduced to rubble—that is, "pacified". (Re: 29) However, according to Prouty, Thompson's could be interpreted either Diem's way or, the U.S. Forces way and, that's exactly what happened. As a result, Diem had one view, the State Department had a view that was similar to Diem's and the Department of Defense had a completely different view (or, was it as I suspect, *the CIA's view?*). If you recall, the Department of Defense had assigned a MAAG unit in South Vietnam *to advise* the newly created ARVN. The CIA had control of the SMM in South Vietnam. This is how things stood until 1963, and the assassination of JFK.

Author's Notes: I believe that at the time of JFK's death, there were about 12,000 military advisors assigned to MAAG. How many personnel were assigned (or attached) to the SMM is unknown to me (or to anyone else for that matter!) What is known is that "General" Lansdale with unlimited money, power, and influence, had one objective in mind: *Place and keep Diem in power*! He did this with the CIA's army! Not only did he have access to the U.S. Military i.e.: Army and Naval units but also had the money to hire thousands of Filipino mercenaries, many of whom he had successfully led against the HUK uprising in the Philippines.

In retrospect, it is obvious that the whole idea of a democratic government in South Vietnam was built on "shifting sand"; *it never had a chance.* According to Higgins (*Our Vietnam Nightmare*), Diem made a valiant effort to bring reform and prosperity to his beleaguered nation. Constant strife within and mixed messages from without i.e.: The U.S., made it impossible. When Diem became frustrated, he struck out on his own doing what he thought was right as opposed to what Washington thought was right.

Of course, this created major problems for him. While some thought he was doing the right thing, others thought he was doing the wrong thing. What developed was a "Diem must go" camp. Others, although not happy with the situation, believed that getting rid of Diem would result in irreparable harm to the whole Vietnamization program. Thus, a Diem-must-stay camp developed.

In general, the Diem-must-go camp consisted of member of the State Department lead by Averell Harriman, the Under Secretary of State for Political Affairs and Roger Hilsman, the Assistant Secretary for Far Eastern Affairs. The Diem-must-

Re: 29 Ibid., pg. 250

stay camp was composed of members of the Department of Defense and the CIA. Among the "stay" group were Robert McNamara, Secretary of Defense and General Maxwell Taylor, Chairman of the Joint Chiefs-of-Staff. Within the CIA, I would include its director, John McCone. In addition to those mentioned on both sides, I would include the President on the "go" side and the Vice President (Johnson) on the "stay" side. I believe that Johnson was a very strong advocate of the Diem-must-stay camp. Another whom I believe *must* be put in the "stay" camp was Edward Lansdale! Why Ed Lansdale? I believe that I have established that the CIA had a tremendous investment in the affairs of South Vietnam which, without any doubt in my mind, put them firmly in the "Diem-must-stay" camp. After all, Diem was the "CIA's man" and Lansdale, the *instrument* of the CIA, had successfully installed Diem as President. Consequently, both the CIA *and* Lansdale had the most to lose if Diem were to go.

Author's Notes: What I want to do now is remind the reader of Lansdale's *close*, personal relationship with members of the Filipino army. This is the same army that, under the leadership of Lansdale, had defeated the HUK insurgency, and successfully installed Magsaysay as President of the Philippines. His success was die to his expertise in counterinsurgency tactics and the employment of "vintage" Filipino scouts! In South Vietnam, we know that they were paid CIA mercenaries *but* were other promises made?

We all know that the "Diem-must-go" faction prevailed so, let's look at some of the more influential people in that camp; people who were not well known to the public but were trusted advisors to the President.

One, already mentioned, was Averell Harriman. Harriman was a career diplomat with a long history of dedicated public service. Harriman had been appointed by the President to be his special emissary to Moscow to "broker" a nuclear test-ban treaty with the Soviets and to help bring about a peace accord in Laos. Harriman had been *somewhat* successful at both. As far as Vietnam was concerned, early on he had serious doubts about whether a military solution in that country was possible. He was also concerned about the corruption he perceived in the Diem regime and privately urged the President to disassociate himself and the U.S. from him. Another key player in the "go" camp (and also, already mentioned) was Roger Hilsman.

Hilsman was a career intelligence officer. After graduating from West Point, in 1943, he joined (or was recruited by) the Office of Strategic Services (OSS), the fore-runner of the CIA. According to some sources, during World War II, he operated behind the Japanese lines in Asia along with other army and OSS personnel. Other sources place him with Merrill's Marauders in the China-Burma Theater of operations. Roger had earned the respect and confidence of the President and he was often called upon to perform special assignments for him. Hilsman considered himself an expert in guerrilla operations and tactics and perhaps, that was the reason that Kennedy chose him to accompany Michael Forrestal, a member of the White House National Security Staff, to go to Vietnam on a fact-finding mission. Forrestal once described Hilsman as a "very sharp and outspoken person who had a knack of driving the military up the wall." (Re: 30) This may have been true since it was known that, at least on one occasion, the military refused to attend a meeting unless Hilsman was barred from attending it. Whether it was known or unknown to Hilsman, i.e.: Intentional or not, he will play an important role in the timing of Diem's assassination.

To believe that Harriman and Hilsman were the only two within the State Department who wanted Diem "to go" would be a false conclusion. I believe that there were many others *throughout* the Kennedy Administration who thought that it was time to replace Diem—*even the President himself!* However, I do not believe that any of them wanted to see Diem assassinated. As-a-matter-or-fact, the evidence is clear that ample arrangements were made to *insure* that Diem's family were safely removed from the country. (The fact is: That they were safely aboard the aircraft that was to evacuate them when, at the last minute, Diem and his brother, decided to get off and return to the palace; a mistake that resulted in their murder)

What must have been the mood of the "stay" camp when they learned of Diem's assassination? Shock for certain! (even the President was dismayed). Was shock followed by resentment? I think so. I believe that, as a result of Diem's assassination, a-call-it-what-you-will camp ("get even", "revenge") surfaced. I believe that the camp was small *but powerful*. I believe that the nucleus of this camp was buried somewhere within the CIA. What makes me believe that? Simply this: (1) they "recruited" Diem to be president, (2) they "bought out" the leaders of the warring factions in the South, (3) out of the warring factions, they created an army to support Diem, (4) they trained that army, and (5) they relocated over a million Vietnamese from the North to the South in order to give Diem a "constituency" to support him.

Re: 30 Kennedy In Vietnam by William Rust, DaCapo Paperback, 1985, pg. 67

I believe that the assassination of Diem only *fueled* the rift between the CIA and Kennedy that had begun with the failure of the Bay of Pigs. *I believe that someone decided that it was time for JFK to go!*

Chapter Three

That other forces were at work inside South Vietnam clambering for the removal of Diem

Another element that I will put in the "go" camp was the Voice of America. Again, we will see later the role or influence that the VOA played. In the meantime, a little background on the United States Information Agency (USIA).

The USIA was founded in 1953, as an independent agency of the U.S. Government. Its director is appointed by the president and is subject to Senate approval. The mission of the agency is to act as a liaison, exchanging information on policies between the United States and other foreign countries of the world. The type of information exchanged will normally fall into the category of "official" government information releases. In other word, we can say that the USIA is the "official mouthpiece" of the U.S. Government.

In addition to policy announcements, the USIA also administers education and cultural international exchange programs. Much of this is accomplished through the VOA, which "airs more than 1300 hours of programming each week in English and 42 foreign languages to an estimated 120 million listeners around the world. The agency maintains more than 200 posts in 127 countries. Its main headquarters is in Washington, D.C." (Re: 32)

The VOA was actually founded during WWII, primarily as a propaganda "machine" and was widely utilized in the preparation for the invasion of Europe and thereafter until the end of WWII. The VOA also played a major role during the Cold War.** One of its major objectives was aimed at creating discontent within the Soviet Bloc nations. In this respect, it enjoyed some major successes. One was in October, 1956, when in Budapest, Hungary, nearly a quarter-million people took the streets to protest communist rule and demand freedom. When the situation got out of hand for the local communist government, they called on the Soviet Union for help. As a result, Soviet troops and tanks moved in to quell the rebellion. The lucky freedom fighters escaped through Austria who courageously opened their borders to them. Many were quick to say that the VOA had lead them to believe that once the revolt had begun, American troops (already station in West Germany) would rush to their aid and, in effect, invade Hungary.

Re: 32 Encarta, Electric Encyclopia.com

** See my comments on VOA and its relationship to Radio Free Europe (RFE) on the next page.

Of course, any overt action by American forces was simply out of the question. Never the less, the implication was that the VOA "incited" those freedom fighters in Hungary to action.

Author's Note: I remember will those days following the Hungarian uprising. Thousands of refugees crowded into Austria and created a real problem for the Austrian authorities. Many of them wee brought to the United States and "housed" at Camp Kilmer, in New Jersey, where they were debriefed by Army CIC agents. All-in-all, they were a "goldmine" of intelligence information for our forces. In addition, efforts to assimilate them into our society was immensely successful. I say that I remember it well because, in 1956, late in the year, I passed through Kilmer on my way to an assignment in Europe. At the time, I was not yet in intelligence work but later, after my assignment in CIC duties, I met several agents who participated in the debriefing operation. Without a doubt, they all came away from that operation with a sense of accomplishment. A virtual cornucopia of valuable intelligence information was collected with considerable ease.

I hope that I have not "lost" my reader in taking the above diversion away from the "Go" Camp. I felt the need to demonstrate the power and influence of VOA so that you can better appreciate its role in shaping the events in Saigon that ultimately lead to the assassination of Diem. The connection between VOA and Radio Free Europe cannot be dismissed either. Both were under the control of USIA (VOA still is) and both are instruments of propaganda and both generally cover (broadcast-wise) the same areas of interest relative to U.S. Foreign policy—"That's my story, and I'm stuck with it." (Re: 33)

Two other players in "the final solution" were McGeorge Bundy, then assistant to President Kennedy, and Henry Cabot Lodge, the newly appointed ambassador to South Vietnam.

In the case of McGeorge Bundy, a mystery surfaces and centers for the most part, around two National Security Action Memorandum (NSAM) one #263, approved by President Kennedy on October 11, 1963, and the *second*, NSAM #273, signed by *President* Johnson on November 26, 1963, four days after the assassination of President Kennedy. *What is the mystery you ask?*

Re: 33 *Saturday Night Live,* Weekend Edition, NBC Television

The first draft of NSAM #273 was signed by McGeorge Bundy the day before the President was shot!

Author's Notes: The NSAM was "designed" by Bundy to eliminate some of the bureaucratic paperwork that had apparently "choked" communication between the White House and the National Security Council. (NSC). According to Kai Bird, author of *The Color of Truth*, a biography of McGeorge Bundy and William Bundy, the new President hired Bundy to help him "to straighten and to simplify the operations of the National Security Council" (Re: 34) The "A" in NSAM was for "Action" and meant to replace *discussions* in the NSC with *action*.

So, what is so significant about those two NSAMs? Let's see! NSAM #263—*according to many in the know*, contained a blueprint for withdrawal of all American Forces from Vietnam. To begin, Kennedy had let it be known that he was ordering 1,000 of them home by Christmas; the start of a massive withdrawal, including *all CIA personnel*. The target date for that exodus was by the end of 1965. (See next page for copy of NSAM #263)

Please note that in the *second* paragraph, the President has approved "the military recommendations contained in Section 1B, (1-3) of *the* report . . ."

Re: 34. *The Color of Truth* by Kai Bird, Simon & Schuster, NY., 1998

2

THE WHITE HOUSE

WASHINGTON

October 11, 1963

NATIONAL SECURITY ACTION MEMORANDUM NO. 263

TO: Secretary of State
          Secretary of Defense
          Chairman of the Joint Chiefs of Staff

SUBJECT: South Vietnam

At a meeting on October 5, 1963, the President considered the
recommendations contained in the report of Secretary McNamara
and General Taylor on their mission to South Vietnam.

The President approved the military recommendations contained
in Section I B (1-3) of the report, but directed that no formal
announcement be made of the implementation of plans to withdraw 1,000 U.S. military personnel by the end of 1963.

After discussion of the remaining recommendations of the report,
the President approved an instruction to Ambassador Lodge which
is set forth in State Department telegram No. 534 to Saigon.

                                    McGeorge Bundy

Copy furnished:
   Director of Central Intelligence
   Administrator, Agency for International Development

                              cc:
                                  Mr. Bundy ✓
                                  Mr. Forrestal
                                  Mr. Johnson
          TOP SECRET — EYES ONLY   NSC Files

DECLASSIFIED
E. O. 11652, SEC. 3(E), 5(D), 5(D) AND (E)

Committee Print of Pentagon Papers

BY HJ2   NARA DATE 7/15/77

What report? The report that the President was referring to came to be known as the *Trip Report*. The official title of the report was Document 142, "Report of McNamara-Taylor Mission to South Vietnam." Section 1B (1-3) was as follows: (Recommended that:)

1B (1)   General Harkins review with Diem the military changes necessary to complete the military campaign in the Northern and Central area (I, II, and III Corps) by the end of 1964, and in the Delta (IV Corps) by the end of 1965

1B (2)   A program be established to train Vietnamese so that essential functions now performed by U.S. military personnel can be carried out by Vietnamese by the end of 1965. *It should be possible to withdraw the bulk of U.S. personnel by that time.* (my italics)

1B (3)   In accordance with the program to train progressively Vietnamese to take over military functions, the Defense Department should announce in the very near future presently prepared plans to withdraw 1,000 U.S. military personnel by the end of 1963. This action should be explained in low key as an initial step in a long-term program to replace U.S. personnel with trained Vietnamese without impairment of the war effort. (my italics) Re: 35

Author's Notes: There are a number of references to the above three recommendations contained in the Trip Report. There is controversy over 1B (3) as to how and why it was included. The author, Newman (*JFK and Vietnam*) gives creditable evidence that General Taylor (then Chairman, Joint Chiefs) may have included it in order to pressure Diem into making some policy changes. Never the less, we have NSAM #263 *and* the President's approval of 1B (1-3).

Note: It is crucial that you notice who signed NSAM #263—McGeorge Bundy!

Unfortunately, I do not have a copy of NSAM #273, signed by President Johnson on 26 November, 1963, four days after the assassination. (Actually, I am only assuming Johnson signed it) Now, guess who prepared the draft of "273"—exactly, *McGeorge Bundy*. And when did he prepare "273"? The

Re: 35 *JFK and Vietnam,* by John M. Newman, Warner Books, NY., 1992, pg. 402

night before President Kennedy was assassinated! On "263" please note who received "carbon copies" (CC) . . . McGeorge Bundy, Michael Forrestal, and the Vice President! IS SOMETHING GOING ON HERE? Let's see what "273" states. (Thanks to Mr. Newman) (Re: 36)

The *first* paragraph:

"It remains the central object of the United States in South Vietnam to *assist* the people and government of that country to win *their* contest against the externally directed and supported Communist conspiracy."

The *second* paragraph:

"The objectives of the United States with respect to the withdrawal of U.S. military personnel remain as stated in the White House statement of October 2, 1963."

Author's Notes: The White House statement, referenced above, was based on the *judgments* of McNamara and Taylor (in their Trip Report). However, NSAM #263, *left no question* about the withdrawal "order" of President Kennedy. (paragraph 3) This, according to Newman was a "tactic step backward from NSAM-263."

NOTE: At this point and, since we don't have a full context of paragraphs 3, 4, 5, or 6, and, since they are not significant, I want to go to paragraph seven.

Paragraph *seven:*

"With respect to action against North Vietnam, there should be a detailed plan for the development of additional *Government of Vietnam* resources, especially for sea-going activity, and such planning should indicate the time and investment necessary to achieve a wholly new level of effectiveness in this field of action."

NOTE: A reminder to my reader; the foregoing paragraphs are reportedly *draft* paragraphs of NSAM #273 (by Bundy), which as I have pointed out, made a certain changes *in tenor* to JFK's #263. Still, nothing really dramatic *until paragraph seven.*

Re: 36 Ibid, pgs. 439, 440

The draft of paragraph seven seem to reflect President Kennedy's intent i.e.: As in NSAM #263. However, Bundy's final draft of paragraph seven which Johnson approved on Sunday, November 24, 1963, was much stronger:

Paragraph seven:

"Planning should include different levels of possible increased activity, and in each instance there should be estimates of such factors as:

    A. Resulting damage to North Vietnam;
    B. The plausibility of denial;
    C. Possible North Vietnamese retaliation;
    D. Other international reaction.

Plans should be submitted promptly for approval by higher authority." (Re: 37)

This paragraph opened the door for future operations *conducted* by U.S. military forces in South Vietnam!

"A December memorandum for the President, *prepared by Hilsman,* detailing actions that *had "been taken pursuant to NSAM-273"* (my italics), contained this passage:

> A joint CIA—Defense plan for *intensified* operations against North Vietnam, providing for selective actions of *graduated* scope and intensity, is being prepared in Saigon and is due in Washington by December 20th". (Re: 37)

There can be no question that the Johnson Administration ushered in a new era of escalation of the war in South Vietnam. This was now possible as the result of two critical events; the assassination of Diem and President Kennedy. The "Hawks" were now free to win the war in Southeast Asia and prevent the whole of the area from falling under Communist domination. President Johnson was determined that this would not happen during "his watch". This anti-communist psychology emanated out of the "domino" theory; that if one nation fell to Communism, another would follow. A phrase that was often used in this connection was "creeping Communism".

Re: 37 Ibid., pg. 446

In the beginning, Diem had been our hope that—with our help and advice—he could unite all of the diverse political and religious factions together into a "unite front" against the spread of Communism. However, as time went on, it became apparent that he could not "harmonize" the factions; quite the contrary, he did just the opposite. When *advice* was tendered by officials of the Executive Branches of the U.S. and were either rejected, or ignored, frustration "set in". *Diem had to go!*

Author's Notes: In the late 60s and early 70s, I served as a liaison officer to an ARVN Intelligence Battalion. The organization that I was attached to was the Delta Administrative Service Detachment (DASD), 525 Military Intelligence Group, Can Tho`. The Delta was considered critical to the success of winning the war. Consequently, a lot of time, effort, and money went into the intelligence effort. I came away from the assignment with the belief that all of the best-laid plans and advice came to almost nothing.

The ARVN Battalion took our money and our advice and did nothing with it worthwhile. They were prone to ignoring advice and doing just what they wanted to do—just (apparently) as Diem had done with our advice—nothing! For my efforts, I was given an award from ARVN Battalion—which I refused!

And what about President Kennedy? Why was he in the "Diem-must-go" camp?

Author's Notes: Before answering the above questions, I just want to remind the reader that I was an intelligence agent during this period of time, and much of what I have written about *and will* write about, I either had first-hand knowledge of, or, was aware of the Vietnam situation through the media. Having said that, I am relying much on the literature of the Vietnam era since most of it was either *personally* witnessed by the writers, or those writers had access to documents that I have not been privy to. As such, I believe that my knowledge of the "cult of intelligence" and personal knowledge of events affords me the ability to evaluate that information that I cite (and reference) with more credibility than most others who have been more "commercially" popular with their publications. For example, in Vietnam, I served in the Delta, the IV Corps area, the most crucial area of concern for our military experts. *I knew the problem and experienced it first-hand.*

Sorensen, in *Kennedy*, relates the President's concern over the Diem policies:

"By late summer, 1963, he had become more concerned. Growing disunity and disorder within the non-Communist camp in Saigon further handicapped the national war effort . . .

In a long letter to Diem, the President reviewed frankly the troubled relations between the two governments. Some of the methods used by some members of your government, he wrote Diem, may make it impossible to sustain public support in Vietnam for the struggle against the Communists.

Unless there are important changes and improvements in the apparent relation between the government and the people in your country, (the) American public and Congressional opinion *will make it impossible to continue* without change their joint efforts.

The constant rejection of our advisor's advice, Kennedy knew, had made much of our aid and effort useless." (my italics) (Re: 38)

JFK was to make a statement during a press conference, in September, that many believe *directly* ignited the "Diem-must-go" movement. In response to a reporter's question, the President said:

"Diem could regain the support of the people and win the war only with changes in policy and perhaps with personnel . . . . I don't think the war can be won unless the people support the effort and, in my opinion, in the last two months the government *has gotten out of touch with the people*." (Re: 39) (my italics)

And now, for my last "Diem0must-go" personality, Henry Cabot Lodge. In Kennedy's effort to persuade Diem to "make changes and improvements", he "withheld all economic aid not directly related to the battlefront, including Nhu's Special Forces. And he strengthened the authority of new Ambassador Henry Cabot Lodge, the *least friendly* to Diem and family of all the State, Defense, and CIA officials in Saigon, recalling the pro-Diem station chief to Washington. Lodge *urged* dismissal of the Nhus and an *end* to *Diem's arbitrary actions*. (my italics)

Re: 38/39 Ibid pg 658

Author's Notes: I'm trying to remember who the "pro-Diem" station chief was in Saigon who the President recalled. Of course, the station chief in any embassy (and they're in them all) is a CIA employee, so it seemed a little odd that the president himself would actually do the recall. I'm of the opinion that the President ordered the Director, CIA, (John McCone) to do it for him. My dilemma stems from the fact that William Colby was the station chief in Saigon but he was recalled sometime in 1962. He was replaced by John Richardson in March 1962, who was reportedly close to Nhu, Diem's *brother.*

Richardson was replaced in October 1963, therefore, the dilemma is resolved; Richardson was "pro-Nhu" not "pro-Diem" a minor detail I will admit.

Now that the forces in the Diem *stay-vs-go* have been identified, it is time to move from the "cast of characters" on into the "plot" as it is about be written in history. I think that it is important for the reader to note the "tug-of-war" between the "stay" and "go" camp. I.e.: Between the CIA (stay) and the State Department (go).

NOTE: I do not believe for a moment that anyone in the "Diem-must-go" Camp wanted him or his brother murdered. *The same can be said for President Kennedy.*

DIEM STATUS BOARD		
Diem-must-go	Stuck in the Middle	Diem-must-stay
Harriman (State)	Rusk (State)	Lansdale (CIA)
Hilsman (State)	Gen. Harkins (USA)	McCone (CIA)
Kennedy (Pres.)	Gen. Taylor (USA)	Richardson (CIA)
Conein (State)	(Conein) (Switched)	Johnson (V.P. U.S)
Lodge (State)		

"Seek simplicity; then distrust it"

—Alfred North Whitehead

Chapter Four

That another motive for the assassination of the President could have been associated with the "failure" of the Bay of Pigs.

I want to answer one question right off—Do I believe that Oswald shot President Kennedy? The answer is no! Did he take a shot at the President? Quite possibly, after all, there has to be some explanation of the "spent" shells at the location he is alleged to have been when the President was shot. But let me assure my reader, those shells could have gotten there by many means! Yet, the Warren Commission found that the "evidence of Oswald's single-handed guilt is overwhelming". Obviously, I do not believe that! (nor do millions of other Americans!) However, no one will deny that the history books are full of "lone assassins" so much so, that it is *convenient* to conclude that most are done by lone gunmen.

> "For every problem there is a solution which is simple, direct, and wrong."
>
> —H.L. Mencken

There is, in the annals of group behavior, a concept called "Multiple Causality" i.e.: "Most behavior of any significance has multiple causes and multiple consequences." (Re: 40) A classic example was the decision to launch the *Challenger*. "How can you explain why extremely intelligent, caring managers at NASA decided to proceed with the Challenger shuttle launch on a cold January 28, 1986, when, as tragically proven true, the rubber rocket seals would not hold in temperatures below 50 degrees? *Although it is an all-too-human trait to want to find the single villain—a simple cause that explains everything*—a combination of many factors allowed NASA to send astronauts to their deaths while millions watched on TV." (Re: 41) (my italics)

Author's Notes: The failure of the Bay of Pigs is another example of "Multiple Causality". Still, many blamed the President's cancellation of the second air strike (if indeed, *he really was the one who cancelled*) as *the cause* for failure. We see again "the all-too-human trait to find the *single* villain." As a result, we must consider the animosity that was generated (toward the President) as one of the *causal* factors in the decision to assassinate him).

Having explained the concept of "Multiple Causality", I will proceed to address the *issue* of the Bay of Pigs as a motive. I use the word "issue" because the "Cuban" factor was more complicated than the one issue of the "Bay". For

Re: 40/41 *Effective Behavior in Organizations* by Cohen, Fink, Gadon & Willits, 6th Edition, Irwin, (1995), pg. 19

political reasons, Cuba had been made a focal point of U.S. foreign policy. In Part I of this book, I articulated many of those issues, not the least of which was the realization that we had a communist government 90 miles off our coast and it "bugged" the Hell out of us! If you recall, JFK had made a campaign issue out of it. Whether or not the new president had known about it or not (and chose to ignore it), the Eisenhower administration had already addressed the "problem" and had initiated steps to overthrow the Castro regime.

As a-matter-of-fact, Nixon was already aware of those steps but due to secrecy, he was not able to defend the administrations position on Cuba. Consequently, he was constrained from defending either himself or the Eisenhower administration even though he had been one of the most outspoken advocates for action to remove Castro! (Remember, it was not until *after* the election that the President-elect was briefed on the *original* plan at his Palm Beach residence)

One of the causal factors related to Cuba, may have been "Operation Mongoose", a CIA plan designed to overthrow Castro. It is interesting to note that the plan was "activated" after the Bay of Pigs but derived its initial authority from the Eisenhower Administration, possibly in 1960. Operation Mongoose was just another plan to get rid of Castro.

To say that the President took the failure of the Bay of Pigs *personally* is an understatement. Nobody—State, CIA, Department of Defense all—escaped the wrath of the President. Heads rolled, especially that of Richard Bissell, the man in charge of the Cuban exile program. However, most of the "heat" fell on the CIA. There is plenty of evidence in the literature that the President was considering reorganizing the entire intelligence community with the intent of stripping the CIA of its power and influence.

Robert Kennedy, then Attorney General, undertook the task of "marshaling" efforts to remove Castro. To understand the situation better, I quote Sam Halpern, Executive Officer of "Task Force W", the CIA component in the "Get Castro" squad:

"The pressure was on at the CIA, whose anti-Castro operations the Kennedy's held in contempt after the failure at the Bay of Pigs." However, "the people in the CIA saw it differently . . . you don't know what pressure is until you get those two Sons of Bitches laying it on you . . . We felt we were doing things in Cuba because of a family vendetta and not because of the good of the United States." (Re: 42) In other words, the Kennedy's were taking on Castro for personal reasons. "It wasn't national security—it was like their father always said—"Don't get mad; get even!" (Re: 43)

Author's Notes: Sam *Halpern*, not to be confused with Mort Halperin, senior member of the National Security Council. Now, from here on, it would be very easy for me to "stray" afar from the purpose of my writing: causal factors contributing to the decision that the President "must go". Someone has dubbed the intelligence activity as "the web" of intelligence. It is a correct pronouncement. With compartmentation and the norm of never letting the "left hand know what the right hand is doing" *is* what the conduct of intelligence is all about. However, I am going to pursue the Mongoose Operation a little further.

One thing is for sure, the failure of the Bay of Pigs did not end the President's determination to rid the world of Castro. While I don't think that he had assassination of Castro on his mind, the CIA did! As previously indicated, that was the "job" of *Task Force* "W" (but more about that later).

As such, the CIA was ordered to come up with a plan to remove Castro in the summer of 1961. In response, the agency initiated *Operation Mongoose.* Selected to run the operation was the "hero" of the Philippines, Brigadier General Edward G. Lansdale, a "renowned" counterinsurgency expert. Lansdale reported directly to Bundy, the President's national security advisor. As if to "punctuate" the Kennedy determination to "get Castro", Robert Kennedy took a personal interest in the operation and often met with Lansdale and Bundy.

"By February 1962, Lansdale had submitted a detailed, six phase plan, entitled "The Cuba Project", for the removal of the Castro regime by October" (of that year). The report, in part, outlined the goal of fomenting a popular uprising against Castro, however, "guidelines for Mongoose—approved by Bundy *and*

Re: 42 *The Dark Side of Camelot* by Seymour M. Hersh, Little, Brown & Company, NY 1997, pg. 269

Re: 43 Ibid pg. 269

the President, made it clear that final success will require decisive U.S. military intervention." (Re: 44) (my italics)

What happened to "Mongoose"? Some "hit-and-run" operations were actually carried out by special military teams—probably Navy Seals—some fields and crops were destroyed and some attempt at mining of Harbors—for all the "hoop-la", the operational goal was a failure.

On July 25, 1962, Lansdale reported to Bundy and the Special Augmentation Group (SAG) that the JCS had "fully met its responsibility under the March guidelines for planning and undertaking actions for a decisive U.S. capability for intervention in Cuba." (Re: 45)

By August (1962), Bundy was receiving such alarming information about the Soviet military shipments to Cuba that a new track for direct military intervention—separate from Mongoose—was initiated. (Re: 46) In other words, Operation Mongoose was effectively—*killed!* Could the new initiative been "Task Force W"? No. Task Force W was initiated about the same time as "Mongoose" but its purpose was the *elimination* of Castro (as opposed to simply overthrow him). At this point no one believed that any amount of pressure from the inside or outside of Cuba would be enough to convince the dictator to "flee" the island.

Author's Notes: Before going any further, let's recap three causal factors that could have lead to the decision to assassinate JFK: *One,* the failure of the Bay of Pigs which the President took responsibility for (and was ultimately blamed for), *two*, was the decision to eliminate *Operation Mongoose*, and *three*, was retaliation for the assassination of Diem, which the President *tacitly*, at least, allowed to happen.

We know from the Church Committee's findings that plans for the assassination of Castro, code name *OrtsaC* (Castro spelled backwards) were actually "put into play". One such plan was *Task Force W*. The concept included the recruitment of the Mafia to deliver instruments of poison to

Re: 44 *Color of Truth,* pg. 242

Re: 45 Ibid pg. 243

one or more members of "the family" in Havana who would then somehow "slip" Castro a poison "mickey". Of course, the plan failed—if for no other reason that no one could get close enough to deliver it. Another failure!

Another plan was codenamed ZF/RIFLE; its concept was to assassinate Castro using long-range rifles! Another Failure! Would these attempts not be enough to cause Castro to also want JFK "out of the way"? I think so. So let's add another factor to the "assassination equation".

Perhaps one of the most "creative" concepts to dislodge Castro from power . . . began when "Bundy passed on to Lansdale a memo written by a *friendly* (my italics) congressman suggesting yet another military operation:

The invasion by Free Cuba forces (with U.S. logistical support) of the Isle of Pines, a sparsely populated 1,100-square-miles off the southwest coast of Cuba. Having "liberated" a piece of Cuban territory, the émigré force would declare itself the rightful government of all Cuba. Washington could extend recognition to a new Cuban government. This, in turn, would give the Kennedy administration legal cover to defend this piece of "free" Cuba by imposing a blockade against Castro's regime on the main island. Bundy like the idea . . . (Re: 47) (See Figure 4-1)

Re: 46/47 Ibid pg. 243

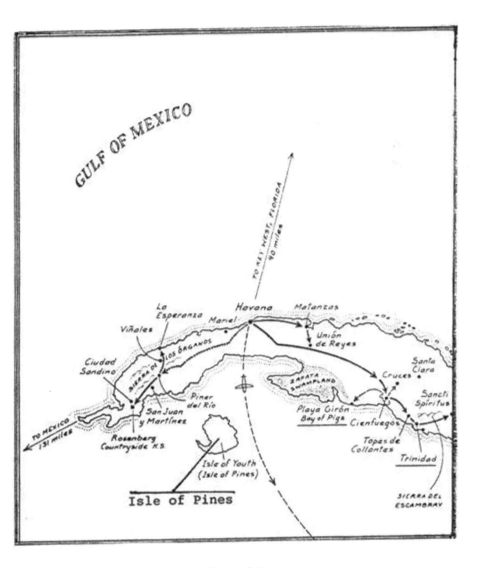

Figure 4-1

Author's Notes: Before moving on, I want to call the reader's attention to the afore-mentioned plan to try and poison Castro and the subsequent "recruitment" of the Mafia Forces. The reason I want to do this is to again, demonstrate that there is a *dual* governmental framework within our Constitutional framework; a sub government (if you will) that acts *always* behind the scenes of our "legal" system. The example I want to use in this case has to do with the use of the Mafia. According to most reliable resources, Bobby Kennedy, then the Attorney General, the one who publicly pursued the Mafia with a vengeance either suggested, or knew and approved the use of the Mafia in the Kennedy effort to "get" Castro. I understand that he later denied this but—who wouldn't? Personally, I believe it. However, one might ask why the Mafia could be so easily persuaded to engage in such an operation. Simple, they wanted to see a "free" Cuba again where they could operate literally, in the open, as they had before the fall of Batiste. Yes, Cuba had been an important base of operations for them during the Batiste years (Batiste was "on the payroll").

/-/-/-/-/-/-/-/-/

When did all of this activity against Castro come to and end—and—why? Recall that in August, 1962, Bundy was getting intelligence reports of Soviet military shipments to Cuba. What followed in October, 1962, was the Cuban Missile Crisis! To our horror, the Soviets had installed 42 missiles with ranges of 900—to over 2,000 miles! (Each with a nuclear warhead). Suddenly, well, almost, Washington, DC., New York, Chicago, Los Angeles, and every city in between, was "in range" of destruction. Fortunately, for us, the Soviets maintained control of all of those missiles. As Khrushchev was to recall "Castro suggested that in order to prevent our nuclear missiles from being destroyed, we should launch a preemptive strike against the United States. In other words, we needed to immediately deliver a nuclear missile strike against the United States. When I read this, I, and all of the others, looked at each other, and it became clear to us that Fidel totally failed to understand our purpose . . . We had installed the missiles *not* (my italics) for the purpose of attacking the United States, but to keep the United States from attacking Cuba." (Re: 48)

Author's Notes: For whatever Americans might think of Khrushchev, I think that it is apparent that he exercised sound judgment and strategy. (Also, I found it very disturbing that Castro was ready to unleash those weapons of mass destruction against us). We shall see how his strategy influenced JFK to take action that can be included in the causal factor's list for assassination.

Again, there is a lot of "hoop-la" about what the President did to "make the Soviets back down". This is just another example of what we, Americans, were told (opposed to what actually occurred). While all of the "talk" about forcing the Soviets was being broadcast through the media, something else was going on behind the scene. However, before I do that, I want to point out one more example of what I have referred to as "intelligence being a high stakes game." No less than the Soviet leader himself, Nikita Khrushchev!—"Concerning our intelligence agents, who had informed us about the invasion, it might have been possible that *this information was planted for them to find.* (my italics) *The American intelligence agents knew our agents. I think there are tactic exchanges of this kind,* where each agency tosses out ideas to the other when one side would like to make sure the other receives something important". (my italics) (Re: 49)

What actually happened is what, in Asian culture, they would call "saving face". JFK, with the help of his brother, Bobby, engaged in something that is known as "back-channeling"; this is very much like when you want to tell your neighbor something and you don't want anyone else to know about it, you sneak out your backdoor, go to your neighbor's house and go in his backdoor.

While the President was playing "hardball" with the Soviets in the media (and for the public consumption), Bobby, along with others at State, wee quietly negotiating with the Russian a solution that would be acceptable to both sides; one in which the President could "claim victory"—*but at a price.* The result of those "back-channeling" negotiations was as follows:

For the Americans:

— Removal of all missiles and their nuclear warheads.
— Permission of the Soviets for U.S. Aircraft to conduct over-flights of Soviet ships to verify the removal of the missiles.

Re: 48/49 *Khrushchev Remembers*: (The Glasnost Tapes), Edited by Schecter with Luchkov, Little, Brown & Co., Boston (1990), pg. 177

For the Soviets:

— A promise by JFK not to invade Cuba (made public).
— Removal of all U.S. missiles from Turkey. (not made public)
— Removal of all U.S. missiles from Italy. (*not* made public)

Here we have the crux of another factor that could have an influence on the assassins to kill the President. The President himself must have known the possible danger to himself and his political future if it ever became known that part of the agreement included removal of missiles from Turkey and Italy. Again, we have Khrushchev's recollection: The president told him through his brother (Bobby)—"If this leaks into the press, I will deny it. I give my word I will do this, but this promise should not be made public". (Re: 50) For Kennedy, *it was a victory*—the missiles were removed and the world was spared a nuclear war. For Khrushchev, it was *also* a victory—Cuba, the communist "nest-egg" in the Western Hemisphere, was safe *and* missiles in Turkey and Italy, poised in the direction of the Soviet Union, were removed. Khrushchev's willingness to "allow" Kennedy to proclaim the victory demonstrated his desire to avoid a nuclear war with the U.S. and the total devastation that would ensue.

In this context, we cannot ignore the fact that the Soviet Leader *also* put *his* life and political future *on the line.* (he was "ousted" in '64, and died a natural death in 1971)

There can be little doubt in my reader's mind that JFK's promise *not* to invade Cuba either directly "or through proxies" created great consternation among members of the CIA, the military, (some) in the State Department, and last but certainly not least, the Cuban exile community. Can there be any doubt that, among these organizations, there were those who were angry enough to want JFK "out of the way"?

Author's Notes: After the Bay of Pigs fiasco, President Kennedy met with Gen. Eisenhower at Camp David on April 22, 1961, for Ike's take on the operation. (See his notes on the following pages)

Re: 50 Ibid pg. 179

NOTES BY GENERAL EISENHOWER ON LUNCHEON MEETING,
APRIL 22, 1961, WITH PRESIDENT KENNEDY AT CAMP DAVID.

(I talked with Allen Dulles the previous day, at the President's
suggestion.)

Mr. Kennedy met me when I landed from the helicopter
at Camp David.   We went to the terrace at Aspen Cottage to talk.
He began by outlining the Cuban situation, including a description
of the planning, the objectives and the anticipated results.   This
outline agreed exactly with that given me by Allen Dulles yesterday
morning.

He explained in detail where things began to go awry and
stated that the whole operation had become a complete failure.
Apparently some men are still hiding in the "bosque" and possibly
have made their way to the mountains.   Apparently about 400
prisoners were taken.

The chief apparent causes of failure were gaps in our
intelligence, plus what may have been some errors in ship loading,
timing, and tactics.

It appears that too much specialized equipment was carried in a single ship and, when this ship was damaged, the troops on the beach were left fairly helpless. I inquired whether or not the troops had had the equipment immediately with them (in platoons and companies) to establish effective road blocks on the three avenues of entry into the swamp area. He was under the impression that this equipment was properly distributed and the troops well trained in its use. Therefore the reason for the quick penetration of the swamp into the vulnerable beachhead was unknown.

The press has mentioned a great deal about MIGs. The President is not certain, and neither was Allen Dulles, that these were MIGs. They could easily have been T-33s, equipped with rockets and guns; but, at least, they shot down a number of our airplanes and apparently operated effectively against our troops in the beachhead.

- 3 -

He is having General Taylor come to Washington to analyze all phases of the operation, including all of the planning and the methods so as to see whether there are lessons to be learned. He has the feeling that we can be faced with some similar situation over the next decade and thinks we should do our best to be prepared to meet it. (He did not say that this report would be made public -- but I did get the impression that it would.)

The next thing that he wanted to talk about were the direction and prospects for future action. I was unable to give him any detailed suggestions, but did say that I would support anything that had as its objective the prevention of Communist entry and solidification of bases in the Western hemisphere.

He believes that the two great powers have now neutralized each other in atomic weapons and inventories; but that in numbers of troops, and our exterior communications as opposed to the interior communications of the Communists, we are relatively weak.

- 4 -

He did not seem to think that our great seapower counteracted this situation completely.

The only real suggestion I could give him regarding the Western Hemisphere was to do his very best to solidify the OAS against Communism, including a readiness to support, at least morally and politically, any necessary action to expel Communist penetration. I said that this was something that had to be worked on all the time. I told him, also, that I believed the American people would never approve direct military intervention, by their own forces, except under provocations against us so clear and so serious that everybody would understand the need for the move.

The President did not ask me for any specific advice. I contented myself with merely asking a few questions about the tactical action, including the timing of the support that I understood the Navy Air had given to the landings. He said that in the first instance they were so anxious to keep the United States hand concealed that they accorded no such support, and when they finally did get word

- 5 -

of its need it was too late. This situation was complicated by the
fact that all communications went out. I understood that the
communication equipment was on the ship that sank, but this is
hard to believe because each unit carries some light communication
equipment, including the ability to send radiograms to a distance
of some fifty to a hundred miles.

There are certainly factors, now unknown, that will
finally come to light under searching scrutiny. The purpose of
this scrutiny is not to find any scapegoat, because the President
does seem to take full responsibility for his own decision, but
rather to find and apply lessons for possible future action.

*   *   *   *

The President brought up Laos. He outlined the situation
and said that the British were very reluctant to participate in any
military intervention and of course the French positively refused to
do so. He thinks that both the British and the French would like
to see Souvanna Phouma brought back to power as the only man

- 6 -

who could possibly maintain and sustain a neutral position in Laos.
(As I remember, our own general opinion, which we had formed
before January 20th, was that Souvanna Phouma had gone so far
toward the Soviets that he could scarcely extract himself from
their clutches.)

The President was quite sure that there was no
possibility of saving Laos by unilateral military action.   Consequently he looked forward to a ceasefire, which is promised for
this coming Monday, the 24th.   He remarked that he was not so
much concerned about Laos as Thailand.   I replied that, in that
event, it would seem the part of wisdom to begin immediately the
strengthening of the Thai forces and positions.   My former reports
led me to believe that the Thai might be very sturdy soldiers
whereas obviously the Laotians didn't like to fight.   I asked him
whether the ICC was to be allowed, coincidentally with the ceasefire, to survey the whole country and see exactly what the situation
was.   He said our people would insist upon that.

SECRET

- 7 -

Again I told him that from my own position I could not
offer any advice -- I could just say that as a generality in order to
keep your position strong at the conference table you had constantly
to let the enemy see that our country was not afraid. We believe
in what is right and attempt to insist upon it.

* * * *

Quite naturally a conversation such as this had no
definite conclusion. We talked throughout most of the luncheon,
and afterward strolled through the camp and continued discussing
various aspects of each situation, but nothing of a dramatic character
came up.

Finally we met with a group of newspaper reporters and
photographers in front of Aspen Cottage. I enjoyed meeting so
many of my old friends among the crowd. He made a very short
statement and said that he had just outlined for me the situations in
these two parts of the world and had asked for my counsel. Nothing
else was said.

SECRET

When the reporters turned to me I said that it was
rather fun to be in the position of not having to make a statement
and having nothing to say.   They then asked me whether I supported
him.   I repeated a generalization that I had expressed on other
occasions -- that when it came to problems of foreign operations,
then an American traditionally stands behind the Constitutional
head, the President.

This of course was said with respect to purposes; no one
outside government is committed to support details of timing,
tactics, selection of operation sites and methods.   These are
not even yet known to outsiders.

After all this, he took me in his car to the heliport and
suggested a golf game in the near future.   Dick Flohr was driving
and John Campion was riding in the front seat.

Chapter Five

That another motive for the assassination of JFK could have his intention to withdraw all troops from Vietnam after the 1964 election.

By July 1962, General Harkins, the U.S. military commander in South Vietnam, stated that "we are on the winning side." (Re: 51) Even though some of the programs, such as the Self-Defense/Hamlet one, was in trouble, the general, in effect, predicted the eventual victory over the VC forces in the south. In particular, Harkins was pleased with improvements in the Delta. Harkins added that "some of the attacks in the Delta were not VC initiated but the acts of bandits that had been operating in the South for thousands of year."

Author's Notes: Just to remind the reader that I served in *the* intelligence unit in the Delta (Delta Administrative Service Detachment) DASD, a "cover" organization in the 525 Military Intelligence Group, in the late 60's and Early 70's as a Liaison Officer to an ARVN Intelligence Battalion. On several occasions, I had the opportunity to visit villages deemed "pacified" by CORDS personnel (Civil Operations and Revolutionary Development Support). My visits were always "coordinated" by CORDS so that I never went alone to the village (not that I wanted to!)—always in the company of one of *their* advisors. I must tell you that my time in the village made me very nervous. The purpose of my visit was to ascertain the value of the intelligence effort of ARVN counterpart i.e.: The unit we were advising. Incidentally, the CORDS program was supported by both the military *and* the CIA. (the military *was* evident, the CIA *wasn't*) Results were "mixed" and I sensed an uneasy peace in the villages that I visited. For one thing, the "mayor" was almost always very youthful and I marveled at how such a young person could gain the confidence of the people.

Let's look for a moment at General Harkins claim that some of the attacks in the Delta were acts of bandits operating in the South "for thousands of years." There is actually some foundation for this statement (whether it goes back thousands of years, I do not know). When Vietnam was divided by the Geneva Agreement in 1954, it allowed for relocation of people from the North to migrate to the South (and visa versa). Estimates range from one to fifteen million Tonkinese (mainly "Catholic") were evacuated to the South—and into the Delta. There is considerable doubt as to how many of those Tonkinese *really* wanted to go south. The real decision as to who would relocate was probably made by the Saigon Military Mission (SMM)—and under Lansdale's direction.

Re: 51 *JFK & Vietnam,* by John Newman, pg. 287

The "dumping" of these "refugees" in and around the Delta created economic havoc in the South and forced the ethnic Cochin Chinese to forage for their food. Many turned to banditry, hence, the General's claim was partially true. So the question to be answered is: How many of the attacks in the South were acts of bandits vs Viet Cong? The answer: *It didn't matter! Every* attack was reported by the SMM as a Viet Cong (VC) attack!

Having validated the General's statement (somewhat anyway), I thought that it was important to do that as well as give the reader some background. Let's turn now to the Summer of 1962.

Following the President's orders to evaluate the situation, the Secretary of Defense took action. Armed with Top Secret briefings and other reports of progress (all at odds with reality), he "ordered a plan be drawn up by the CICPAC (Commander-in Chief, Pacific) for "eventual" withdrawal of all American forces from Vietnam." (Re: 51)

In reality, the plan for executing the U.S. withdrawal was based on three assumptions:

"One, that the insurgency would be under control within three years, two, that U.S. support would be necessary during that time, and, three, that current funding ceilings could be raised." (Re: 52)

Meanwhile, in Vietnam, a virtual "counter-insurgency" began within the U.S. Army. It involved General Harkins, commander of MACV (MAC Vee), Military Assistance Command, Vietnam, and Lt. Col. John Paul Vann, U.S. Army advisor to the South Vietnamese Army.

Author's Notes: If there was ever a hero to emerge from the Vietnam War, it was John Paul Vann. He was a feisty, fiery, perfectionist; fear was an unknown word to him. As advisor to IV Corps, (South Vietnamese Force Area in the Delta), he became a living legend; exhorting his Vietnamese "charges" to "Follow me!" As I have mentioned before, my intelligence unit was in Can Tho, the IV Corps Center and Vann's quarters was located in

Re: 51 *JFK & Vietnam,* by John Newman, pg. 287

Re: 52 Ibid pg. 288

Can Tho. Vann was killed in a Helicopter crash in 1972, while "leading" an attack. Vann was also an invited "guest" at President Kennedy's funeral. Vann's "strength" was that he was a recognized expert on, and in, Vietnam. Almost from the beginning, he was an outspoken critic about how the war was being waged. A book, *A Bright Shining Lie,* by Neil Sheehan, and (I believe) a movie of the same name, details his life and exploits. (Recommended reading)

Of my readers who were ever in the military, have you ever heard of a Lt. Col. "butt" heads with a general? I will say—none of you have! However, that is just what Vann did. He "took on" General Harkins! What could possibly create a mental set in the mind of a "junior" officer to motivate him to hold his top commander in such contempt? First, it was the shocking and often the lack of combat readiness of the South Vietnamese Army *and its commanders.* Secondly, it was the *lack* of will on the part of ARVN commanders to fight; to engage in VC in *mortal combat* and thirdly, it was the refusal of General Harkins to recognize or accept the reality of the first two reasons, i.e.: Harkins existed in a fantasy world devoid of the reality of the deplorable way the war was being conducted. In order to focus attention on all of the above, he chose the Battle of Ap Bac to vent his frustration. The battle of Ap Bac, later identified only as "Bac", began on 2 January 1962. (See Map 5-1)

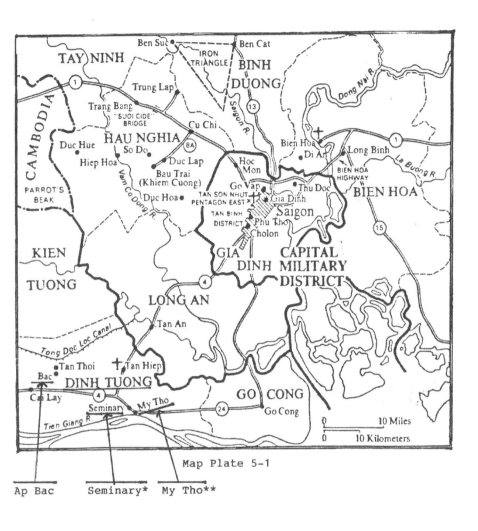

Map Plate 5-1

Ap Bac   Seminary*   My Tho**

---

*   The IV Corps, U.S. Army Advisors leased this former Catholic School to use
      as its living quarters (located about three kilometers outside of My Tho)
**   Prior to an increase in Advisors, they leased a house in My Tho. The house they
      vacated is the one in which members of our intelligence detachment (DASD)
      moved into; the house that I have already mentioned that I visited many times
      in the Late 60's and Early 70's.

Author's Notes: All of my visits to My Tho were made by jeep, over and through acknowledged VC territory. Most of the time, there were two officers (including myself) and one driver.

Our only protection were three M-16 Army rifles. (Murphy's Law of Combat: "Remember that the rifle you are carrying was made by the lowest bidder.") The M-16 rifle that I had no confidence in!

The Battle of Ap Bac could have been a huge success for ARVN forces. The operation was perfectly planned but poorly executed: It could have been a classic Infantry School (Ft. Benning) operation involving a combination air assault and ground forces in the attack, but . . . anything that *could* go wrong *did* go wrong. The element of surprise was missing . . . the ARVN forces "froze" in the attack . . . the coordinated effort between the members of the Civil Guard and ARVN forces was dis-coordinated (The Guard was the first to reach the objective and, as a result of the lack of support from the ARVN, they suffered heavy casualties). The U.S. helicopters ferrying ARVN troops to the objective landed too close to the target area and suffered the loss of five helicopters (Vann told them to land 300 yards from the objective—out of range of *accurate* rifle fire—they ignored the orders and laded within 200 yards away) . . . the planned artillery fire overshot the target. In the end, ARVN forces allowed the VC to escape into the jungle. Vann was furious. Even so, Harkins declared it a *victory!*

As a result, Vann and his superior, Colonel Porter, prepared a scathing "After Action Report" accusing the South Vietnamese of cowardness. The report reached the Pentagon and . . . Harkins's reputation was ruined. He was relieved of command shortly thereafter (and earned the nickname "General Blimp"). Vann, himself, rotated from Vietnam in April 1963. This was not unusual because the "tour" of Vietnam was 13 months (the same as mine). Vann retired from the Army in approximately July 1963. (However, he was to return to Vietnam in a civilian capacity, in 1965).

To carry this tale of distortion and deception further, I call your attention to the case of Sam Adams, a rather obscure (sorry, Sam) intelligence analyst deep in the "belly" of the CIA infrastructure. Sam was hired by the Agency in 1963, and for a time worked in the "Congo" section.

Later, possibly in 1965, he was transferred to the Vietnam section where he began to analyze information gleaned from captured Viet Cong documents relative to the morale and strength of VC forces in the South. To his shock and amazement, he discovered a gap of at least 50% between what the military was reporting the strength of VC forces and what he had reasonably determined from captured documents their strength to be. For example, the military estimated VC strength at approximately 270,000 . . . whereas Adams found it to be more than twice those numbers.

Alarmed, Adams made several attempts to report the corrected VC strength to his top CIA supervisors (who discredited the figure) then, the Pentagon top brass (without success), and then, even to the President (without success). He even attended a conference on war in Honolulu, in 1967, where he was literally ridiculed by the top Pentagon brass. Of course, Adams was virtually vindicated with the advent of the Tet Offensive in 1968. One of the most interesting "findings" of Adams was that there were more than 30,000 enemy intelligence agents operating in South Vietnam in the mid-60s. What does all of this mean? To me, it means that *there was* a conspiracy to promote the war between elements of the U.S. military, the CIA, and perhaps even among some members of the White House staff. In fact, there is ample evidence to make the case that this conspiracy—stared in the early 60s—continued throughout the decade into the early 70s. With the assassination of JFK and the presidency falling into the hands of Lyndon Johnson, a "hawk", the military was free to pursue the war in an unabated fashion for the next five years. Again, I ask my reader—could JFK's intention to withdraw all forces from Vietnam have been another causal factor for his assassination? *If not, why not? If yes, who?*

Author's Notes: Before leaving John Paul Vann's story too far behind, I want to point out another coincidence that I shared with him i.e.: other than the fact that I served in the same area (and towns) that he did. That would be that his immediate supervisor—Francis J. Kelly, who was my Battalion Commander in Korea, in the 50's. Col. Kelly and I both served in a tank battalion assigned to the First Cavalry Division along the DMZ. Kelly, a former NY policeman, and advisor to James "Jumping Jim" Gavin of WWII fame. My association with the colonel occurred prior to my assignment to counterintelligence. I was a company commander and Kelly was my CO. Other than being a fine officer, I remember two things about him most.

First, he could "chew butt" better than any officer I ever served with; I mean he was so good at it, the air around him (and the person on the receiving end) would turn "blue". Just being in the vicinity of one of his outburst made everyone cringe. The second thing I remember most is his "famous" phrase when he asked you what went wrong with an operation or mission: "Don't give me the whole symphony, just the last eight bars"! Since then, I have met a few officers who also knew the colonel and they all agreed with my assessment of him. Some of those officers served under him when he commanded the Fifth Special Forces in Okinawa and Vietnam. In Okinawa, he "earned" the nickname "Splash Kelly" because, in air drops, the troops often landed in the ocean.

Earlier, I mentioned Lyndon Johnson as a "hawk" on the war. I am sure that many of my readers are familiar with the aura of dislike that surrounded the Johnson-Kennedy relationship. One instance that clearly provides us an uncontridictory example of this. It occurred on May 9th (or 10th), 1961, at a National Security Council Meeting. Johnson had just returned from a meeting in New York City where he had heard—by radio—that he was going to Vietnam. He was furious because he had no advanced notice of the announcement. Later, at the Council meeting, the President told Johnson that he wanted him to go. *"Johnson refused!* Kennedy replied: *"You're gong tonight . . ."* (Re: 53) (my italics) That was it! Johnson went but, as we shall see, got his revenge.

Author's Notes: My last statement is not intended to directly link Johnson to the assassination plot (not now anyway) but to follow it with an account of his activities in Saigon; activities that is—statements that would embarrass the Kenned Administration.

The story goes that, on the morning of his arrival in Saigon, the Vice President was handed a cable from the Joint Chiefs of Staff (JCS) and addressed solely to him—"information addressee" (only). Not even the Ambassador (Nolting) ever saw it. The message was drafted for the Secretary of State, McNamara, but copied and sent to the Vice President. Interestingly enough, there is no proof that the Secretary *ever approved* the message—or even saw it! In effect, the message implies that Diem be pressured to request U.S. combat troops be sent to Vietnam. Please remember that the JCS are the *top* brass of all the military services.

Re: 53 Ibid pg. 68

Author's Notes: According to Newman's account, Diem had steadfastly refused to have U.S. combat troops in his country but had asked for the military to help train his soldiers. (Re: 54) Keep in mind also that the President was nearing the point of recalling all existing troops already in Vietnam—not commit more! To me, this is ample proof that the U.S. military conspired to *promote* the war in Vietnam. We shall see how Johnson's visit was "choreographed" by those wishing to promote the U.S. war effort. (*Another causal factor?*) Incidentally, I am only citing Newman's account of the Vice President's visit because it is more representative of the "true" facts. There are other accounts of the visit; all allude to the message content but do not raise the question of the suspicious circumstances surrounding the authorization and, or, the approval of it by either McNamara or the President.

Below, I have summarized what can be considered some of the more critical activities of Mr. Johnson:

1. Committed the U.S. to provide helicopters and armored personnel carriers (APCs) for 20,000 more U.S. troops.
2. "Encouraged" Diem to write a letter to the President along with a "shopping list" of what Vietnam's most urgent needs were.
3. Asserted the U.S. readiness to "assist in meeting the grave situation which confronts you" . . . further, "*There are many things* (my italics) the United States is willing to do."
4. Promised publicly to stand "shoulder to shoulder with the South Vietnamese in their fight against communism." . . . and called Diem "the Churchill of Asia." (Re: 55)

Author's Notes: It is clear to me that Newman (*JFK and Vietnam*) believes that there was a conspiracy in evidence in order to get Diem to request 20,000 U.S. combat troops. Whether or not Johnson "was in on it or not" can only be left to pure conjecture. Perhaps he was "maneuvered" into asking Diem to make such a request by his military advisor, Colonel Burris. Since Diem did not want U.S. combat forces *per se* but is precisely how he was "won over"—the U.S. would commit 20,000 combat forces to "train" the ARVN. *Can* you see how the Vice President "redesigned" JFK's foreign policy agenda?

Re: 54 Ibid pg. 70

Perhaps the VP was simply "overcome" by the intensity and the excitement of the moment (in Saigon where he was probably treated like royalty). After all, was he not a man with a big ego and likely to succumb to flattery?

It is clear that Diem did not want more U.S. Combat Forces n Vietnam; he wanted more U.S. military to *train* an anticipated increase of ARVN—perhaps as many as 100,000 more. What followed seems too coincidental not to have been planned. The offer of military personnel to train ARVN forces was made, and Diem accepted. "In it is the hint of Edward Lansdale's hand . . . (General) McGarr* had conveniently provided Johnson and Diem with a compromise on the troop issue; one that parallels *precisely* (my italics) the formula Lansdale had inserted on April 27th, into the Vietnam Task Force Report."(Re: 56)

What Newman tells us next is one of the most intriguing aspects of the Vice President's visit to Saigon: "There is no proof that Johnson was rehearsed for the combat troops decision, but the idea is hard to rule out (and) adding to the intrigue is the fact that Col. Burris was *specifically* (my italics) instructed by persons he calls "the boys in the woodwork" not to discuss the combat troops issue with his own boss, Vice President Johnson." But why? "I was not authorized to, Burris says, because *Diem was a marked man*, and someone who should not deal with this issue. This raises some troubling questions: Who was giving orders to the VP's aide?" (Re: 57)

Author's Notes: Newman's interview with Burris some years later and, of course, after the fact raises several questions. Not only as to who was giving the orders but also—who were the "boys in the woodwork" and who had foreknowledge of Diem's future (as a marked man)? Incidentally, the italics throughout, are mine.

There is ample evidence that the intrigue involving Diem's acceptance was purely of military origin and with CIA knowledge and approval (of an additional 20,000 U.S. combat troops). I am sure that Burris had to have been a competent, intelligent, and "sharp" military officer for him to have been

Re: 55/56 Ibid pg. 72

Re: 57 Ibid pg. 74

---

*   Military Assistance Advisory Group Chief in Saigon

assigned as a military advisor for such a high-ranking member of the U.S. Government i.e.: The Vice President. As such, even thought he was a colonel (not a "super-rank" in the Pentagon hierarchy), he enjoyed super-status and therefore had the authority and the responsibility to put the Vice President's interests above all else. Consequently, he was not subject to the rank structure the same as anyone else. However, as an advisor, he was subject to advice; to make his own decisions about *what* to advise the Vice President. Then, the question becomes—whose advice are we to take? In the matter of Vietnam, it was someone who was considered an "expert" on the region; someone whose opinion Burris would respect. Now, who might that be?

Chapter Six

The real assassins of the President needed a "dupe" to blame for the killing that was in the planning stages. The dupe selected was Oswald.

I want this chapter to unfold in two phases; Phase I will be an exploration of a "new" thought about Oswald's behavior and actions and, associate it with a theory rarely, if ever, considered as a "motive" for his part in the drama that unfolded at Dealey Plaza n that fateful day in 1963. In Phase II, I will take some of the thoughts that I have offered and suggest to you that Oswald's mind may have been controlled by "outside" influences. i.e.: Either brainwashing or post-hypnotic suggestion.

Phase I

The idea that I want to introduce to the reader in this phase is the idea of what I will simply refer to as *mind control*. For years, mind control (or MC, as I will refer to it), along with ESP, has been researched by intellectuals in the field of intelligence; most notably, in Psychology. I will offer a short history of the concept and bring the theory (and practice) up to current study and then, tie it into some thoughts and theories surrounding the events of the 60's.

While the concept of MC has been around for a long time, it was brought to the forefront during (and after) the Korean War. The North Koreans successfully used a form of MC against our POWs; what came to be known as "Brainwashing". All of their POWs were subjected to the process and many succumbed. Given the harsh treatment endured by or troops, it is not hard to understand how and why it happened although, at the time, it was considered an "unforgivable sin" in the aftermath of their repatriation. One result was the creation by the military of the *Code of Conduct*.

The introduction of the *Code of Conduct* by the U.S. Army (in approximately the Mid-50s), was an attempt to "stem the tide" of any soldier who might, in any future conflict, be captured and subjected to what became known as "Brainwashing". After the release of our POWs, it became apparent that many had collaborated with the enemy in order to receive preferential treatment. In addition, they had been subjected to intense "orientations" in communist ideology. As a matter-of-fact, several of our soldiers refused repatriation, deciding to remain "free" in North Korea! Many Americans were horrified that anyone would choose another way of life over the "American Way".

Author's Notes: Part of the repatriation process included an intelligence debriefing. Many soldiers were identified as having collaborated with the North Koreans. As a result, some were tried y an army court and served time. Others, who were cleared were kept under surveillance as long as they remained in the military and were serving overseas where they would come into contact with foreign nationals. The surveillance was "light" and sporadic. On one of my assignments in Europe, in the late 60's, I was assigned the task of a "follow-up" investigation. My "subject" was a senior enlisted man whose face had been partially eaten away by rats (perhaps). After my investigation, I had no qualms in recommending his "release" from further investigation. Case closed!

For those readers who may not be aware, or familiar with the Code, it reads as follows:

1. I am an American, fighting in the forces which guard my country and our way of life. I am prepared to give my life in their defense.
2. I will never surrender of my own free will. If in command, I will never surrender the members of my command while they still have the means to resist.
3. If I am captured, I will resist by all means available. I will make every effort to escape and aid others to escape. I will accept neither parole nor special favors from the enemy.
4. If I become a prisoner of war, I will keep the faith in my fellow prisoners. I will give no information or take part in any action which might be harmful to my comrades. If I am senior, I will take command. If not, I will obey the lawful orders of those appointed over me and back them up in every way.
5. When questioned, should I become a prisoner of war, I am required to give name, rank, service number and date of birth. I will evade answering further questions to the utmost of my ability. I will make no oral or written statements disloyal to my country and its allies or harmful to their cause.
6. I will never forget that I am an American, fighting for freedom, responsible for my actions, and dedicated to the principles which made my country free. I will trust in my God and the United States of America.

/-/-/-/-/-/-/-/-/-/

I can say this with confidence that every "recruit" in the military gets some kind of "Code" orientation—*early on*—probably within a week or two of their service. Is this some form of MC or just a reaffirmation of what we, as Americans, *already know?* Is it possible also, that the "Code" indoctrination was considered a means of *Pre-programming* our troops in the event of their capture and torture? Now, this is the exact point that I wanted to get to . . .

pre-programming . . . or *post-hypnotic suggestion.* I think I am safe in saying that, in intelligence circles, it is called the Manchurian Candidate theory.

The theory derives its name from a "chilling" novel by Richard Condon. (Re: 58) In it, Condon tells a tale of an American POW who was "Programmed" (while a POW) to assassinate a presidential candidate. Of course, the POW was not aware that the post-hypnotic suggestion had been "planted" in his head. The plan was activated with a phone call. In 1962, a movie version was released that starred Frank Sinatra as the "dupe". The story goes that Sinatra obtained the rights to the movie and did not permit its re-release until well after the assassination of President Kennedy. I am sure that readers know that Sinatra and Kennedy were friends during the period before the Kennedy election. I believe that, in retrospect, the alliance between the two was an "accommodation" Kennedy made in order to get the support of Hollywood's elite. After the election, the friendship "cooled" quickly even though his brother-in-law, Peter Lawford, was a member of the "Rat-Pack" of which Sinatra was "Chairman of the board". Never the less, is it possible that the motion picture could have "inspired" some person, or "persons unknown" to assassinate the youthful president?

Author's Notes: I recall seeing the movie, however, at the time I was not a Sinatra fan and I was not overly impressed with it. In addition, post-hypnotic suggestion was something that was only movie and TV "fare". Very few Americans were aware that thought control was a subject of experimentation in the intelligence community. As we shall soon see, the Soviets, CIA, and Army Intelligence were all conduction such research.

Before I go any further, I want to go back and offer an explanation of the term "Brainwashing" and give an example or two. The term is not unknown to any of us in the intelligence community, however, one of the most succinct explanations has been provided by Colonel Allison Ind. in his book, *A Short History of Espionage":* (Re: 59)

Re: 55/56 Ibid pg. 72

Re: 57 Ibid pg. 74

Re: 58 Published in 1952

Re: 59 A Short History of Espionage pg 314

"There is much misunderstanding about the process, for the term suggests a ruthless combination of physical brutality, mysterious stupefaction of the senses, hypnotic suggestion endlessly repeated, and so on. We now know better. It is simply the psychology of salesmanship carried to the utmost extreme, coupled with the creation of an atmosphere for utmost receptiveness: isolation, mistrust of one's own people, and he apparent sincerity of the proponents."

The first example of brainwashing that I want to give, I will turn again to Colonel Ind. (Re: 60) This is the case of George Blake. Blake was a WWII Dutch espionage agent for the allies who provided valuable information under the very noses of the Germans. After the war, he returned to England to a hero's welcome. As a result, he was given a commission in the British Navy, where he served honorably for a few years.

Ultimately, he left the naval service and entered Cambridge where he studied Russian. After he completed his studies at Cambridge, he joined the consular service and was assigned to Seoul, Korea. When the North Koreans overran South Korea, he was captured and brainwashed. After the war, he again returned to England and hailed once more as a hero.

Blake's next assignment was Berlin, which provided him with easy access to Soviet Intelligence. On at least one occasion, Blake was seen making a contact which could not be easily explained. Thereafter, his movements were both tracked and traced. As it turned out, he was caught and sentenced to over 40 years in prison. He had bought into the Communist Doctrine "hook, line and sinker." Blake had been a Soviet agent for 10 or more years.* Colonel Ind traced Blake's "conversion" back to his POW days in a North Korean prison.

Author's Notes: A few years ago, I met Major General Oleg Kalugin, former KGB and Head of the First Directorate (Western Intelligence) who knew Blake well. According to the General, Blake had been providing intelligence to the Soviets since his release from the North Korean POW Camp in 1953!* *Blake proved to be invaluable to the Soviets!* According to Kalugin, Blake's conversion "was easy considering his radical views"! The question that I am asking now is: Was the general the one who Blake was seen with?

Re: 60 Ibid pg. 314

Before I proceed to offer a second, and more "contemporary" example of "brainwashing", I want to identify the types of individuals who are most susceptible to brainwashing, conversion, or, in the intelligence business: Recruitment. First of all, I want to point out that *whoever* is recruited (as in Blake's case—and in all cases), *the recruit is the "dupe".*

"dupe (doop) . . . A person who is the tool of another person or power."

—The American Heritage Dictionary
(New College Edition)

The dupe never knows anything but what you tell him/her. Dupes never know the "big picture". They never know anyone in the organization but their "handler" i.e.: the person who recruited them. Dupes can be anyone who can help you—usually not your average "church-going" character.

- Note the difference in the time span of Blake's Soviet control between Ind and Kalugin's. Who do you think *really* knew?

Re: 60 Ibid pg. 314

Consequently, in most cases, they are temporary, contractual agents. If they are caught, they can only tell what they know—which is usually very little. There are exceptions, a highly placed agent in a "target" organization (such as Blake, Ames, etc) are used until they are no longer of value. The fact that these "contractual" agents know very little is protection for them as well as the recruiting agency (but you can guess who it protects the most!). *Oswald was a dupe!*

So, what kind of a person does a recruiting agent look for? First, any recruiting operation is carefully planned and, hopefully, carefully executed. Experience tells us that there are three (basically) types of motivators for successful recruitment: Money, revenge, and ideology. Money is the weakest; ideology, the strongest (as seen in the case of George Blake). When I say that money is the "weakest", I mean that it is the most unreliable unless it is substantial enough to dramatically improve the individual's life-style; then they become dependent on it. Of course, that will usually "tip off" their superiors that something is wrong and endanger the investigation.

The person who can be converted through ideology is the most dangerous type of spy. Experience (and history) tells us over and over again that people will die for what they believe in.

> "I regret that I have but one life to live to give to my country"
> "Give me liberty or give me death"
> "I cannot, I will not recant"

Saint Paul who lost his head rather than renounce Christ. The list is endless. After ideology, I would place revenge second and greed third relative to reliability.

Author's Notes: In a later chapter, I will "connect" at least one of the above motivators to the assassination of President Kennedy.

My *second* example of mind control is in two parts: brainwashing and hypnotic suggestion. It may be a little far-fetched for some of you but I believe that we have all been brainwashed at one time or another. My subject in this case is television advertising. I believe that most will admit tat TV advertising is compelling. The first thing the advertiser does is select the "target" audience then, the TV program that is most likely to attract that audience. For the "soaps" you will see an array of items that appeal to women; for sports events, beer and exercise equipment; for cultural programs, Mercedes or Lexus. What is their objective? To *sway, convert,* and *"compel"* you to try their product. How do they *compel* you to buy their product? By appealing to your sense of responsibility! Some examples may be:

For Seniors:	Buy our insurance so your loved ones won't have the (Fear) burden of your funeral expenses! "Did you know that Social Security only pays $255!!! "The average funeral Cost over $4,000.00!
The Family Man:	Our security system will protect you and your loved (Fear & ones! (The scene is a suburban home (late at night, Responsibility) of course). A masked man attempts to enter through a window. The wife hears a noise and runs to

	protect a child. BUT with *their* alarm system, the intruder hears the alarm and runs off into the night!
For Men:	Our hair dye will take years off your look! In six weeks (Ego) (using our exercise equipment) you lose those unwanted pounds and have a body-beautiful. (always a beautiful women there to admire the "new" you.
For Women:	About the same as for men. The exceptions are the (Ego) famous female stars who exhibit the "new" you. (Don't forget to read the small print: "Results not typical")

Author's Notes: The above examples of how advertising agencies use psychological arguments to get you to buy or invest in their product demonstrate some of the same arguments that may be used by members of the intelligence community to recruit spies. Once the dupe is "hooked", fear of disclosure keeps them in line. Ego is another psychological force to recruit. The Soviets were very successful in recruiting American enlisted military personnel by offering them a commission in the Soviet Army. Of course, it was superficial; they never commanded troops. If you are in a Top Secret Intelligence group, it was easy to acquire *any* rank as long as it was necessary to perform the operation. I don't believe that I was ever in an intelligence unit that did not have loads of blank military and civilian ID cards. Of course, they were under tight security and only issued to those who had a need for their mission.

Recall, if you will, Col. Ind's explanation of brainwashing:

"It is simply the psychology of salesmanship carried to the utmost extreme . . ."

It may come as a surprise to some, but often, the easiest person to "convert" is an intelligent one. Why is that? Generally speaking, the more intelligent a person is, the more susceptible they are to logic and reasoning. One more point for comparison of Ind's explanation and the advertising on TV:

"coupled with the creation of an atmosphere for utmost receptiveness . . ."

Where is this "psychology of salesmanship" carried out? In the comfort of your own home—*the very target of intruders!* (Better call that security company now—operators are standing by!)

The second kind of mind control (or hypnotic suggestion) may be more foreign to the average reader but it is more demonic. Perhaps five years ago, it became so prevalent in one of our favorite American past-times that the Federal Government stepped in to prohibit it; *the movie theater!* This is what was happening:

Subliminal messages were flashed on the screen in order to get the audience to buy food and drinks at the snack bar. It was impossible for the human eye to catch them, but the subconscious picked up on them causing the patron to get up and buy the product. Another ploy, more obvious, was to release the odor of popcorn in the theater; again, causing the patron to buy popcorn. The demonic aspect of the action was that it seemed virtually impossible for the patron to resist. The question is: Has this kind of psychological mischief *really* stopped, or are we still being bombarded with those messages via the media of film? The only way to be sure would be to examine *every* film frame-by-frame. Yes, it only takes *one* frame to transmit the desired suggestion!

Perhaps the most convincing evidence that post-hypnotic suggestion (mind control) can be effective are examples that most of us have witnessed, either in person, or on television; ex: situations where "master" hypnotists have put their "subjects under", planted a thought or activity in their mind that they are to think or act out when a special operant word is spoken, then, when brought back to consciousness, the "cue" is given and the subjects do what has been planted in their mind. It always amazes me how easily it is done. For the audiences, it is always hilarious, for the "dupe", embarrassing. Experts, in that field, say that you cannot make anyone do anything that they would not ordinarily do; steal or kill for example. When I hear that disclaimer, I always remember an old radio show, "The Green Hornet" which opened with the "Hornet" (in a deep and menacing voice) saying:

"Who knows what lurks in the hearts of men? . . . the Green Hornet knows!"

NO, I, for one, am not convinced; based on what I have seen, heard, and read, *I do* believe that people under the influence of post-hypnotic suggestion *will* do what they are *programmed* to do. (And I am not alone!)

One of the most definitive books ever written on the subject of mind control was *The Search for The Manchurian Candidate: The CIA And Mind Control* by John Marks (NY Times Books), 1979.

In it, Marks tells "the story of the Agency's secret efforts to control human behavior". Much of what Marks wrote about was not new to me. Ever since I joined the U.S. Army's Counterintelligence Corps, I had heard stories from those agents who had been with the Corps years before my recruitment; many of who had served in WWII. I guess I didn't think too much about it at the time because first of all, I didn't believe it and secondly, it wasn't pertinent to what I had been trained to do: protect the U.S. Army, its personnel, facilities, and classified documents against any encroachment by enemy agents, foreign or domestic, for the purposes of espionage, sabotage, or subversion. As you can determine, mind control was not part of my mission. However, research on it was being conducted by the CIA and, I believe, in conjunction with other intelligence services, including certain elements of the U.S. Army.

Getting back to the "Manchurian Candidate . . .", Marks cites the work of Dr. John Gittinger and his association with the CIA in the 1950s and 1960s. Following is a background profile of Dr. Gittinger:

Dr. John Gittinger (Re: 61)

"Dr. Gittinger, Psychologist, conceived the fundamental idea behind the Personality Assessment System, or PAS. Gittinger's insight evolved into a system (PAS) by which cognitive behavior, emotional reaction, perceptual style, and social interaction can be mapped into 12 scalable dimensions, each representing a component of intellectual function. These dimensions, and the technology for mapping into and out of them constitute the Personality Assessment System.

The PAS has its roots in Gittinger's early career as a psychologist at Central State Hospital in Norman, OK (1948-1949). It was there that he began to observe behavioral differences among the patients, which could be linked to differential (ipsitive)* scores on the sub-tests of standardized psychological test instruments. (From) 1950-1978, Dr. Gittinger's professional career and the PAS further developed as he rose to the position of Chief Psychologist of World-Wide Operations for the Central Intelligence."

---

*   Unsupported assertion, usually by a person of standing

Re: 61 Personality Assessment System Foundation

In fact, we can assume that "medical" experiments on humans occurred prior to the 1950's (See Exhibit 6-1)

Now, what about Oswald and the idea that he was acting under some type of mind control? Quite frankly, I had never considered the possibility that Oswald could have been subjected to some sort of hypnotic suggestion which when "triggered" could have resulted in him being at the wrong place at the wrong time; weapon, and all.

What opened my eyes to this illuminating thought was the book, *Rearview Mirror* (Re: 62), by retired FBI agent, William Turner. In it, he explores (with the help of experts in the field of hypnosis) the possibility that the alleged assassin of Robert Kennedy, Sirhan Sirhan, was a victim of "hypnoprogramming". In his book, Turner relates an interview with Dr. Eduard Simson-Kallas, former chief of San Quenton Prison's psychological-testing program. He had interviewed Sirhan in prison and "the more he probed the inmate's mind, the more he became convinced he had been hypoprogrammed to shoot RFK". (Re: 63) Sirhan had related to both the doctor and Turner that after meeting a girl in a coffee shop in a polka-dot-dress who wanted coffee "heavy on the cream and sugar", he blanked out until he was captured at the scene of the assassination. Until that moment, Sirhan asserted that he remembered nothing. The doctor believed that the girl's cream and sugar statement was the trigger.

Now, what about Oswald's assertion in the Dallas Police Station? When asked by a reporter "if" or "why" he shot the President, he said "I didn't kill nobody" (or words to that effect). If he really didn't remember then who could have subjected him to be hypoprogrammed? Of course, we don't know. What we do know is that the KGB did conduct experiments in mind control.

Re: 62 *Rearview Mirror,* by William Turner, Penmarin Books (2001)

Re: 63 Ibid pg. 254

SECRET

THIS DOCUMENT CONSISTS OF 1 PAGE
NO. 1 OF ... SERIES

UNITED STATES
ATOMIC ENERGY COMMISSION

* 1994000061 *
DOE-OP

April 17, 1947

U. S. Atomic Energy Commission
P. O. Box E
Oak Ridge, Tennessee

Attention: Dr. Fidler

Subject: MEDICAL EXPERIMENTS ON HUMANS

1. It is desired that no document be released which refers to experiments with humans and might have adverse effect on public opinion or result in legal suits. Documents covering such work field should be classified "secret". Further work in this field in the future has been prohibited by the General Manager. It is understood that three documents in this field have been submitted for declassification and are now classified "restricted". It is desired that these documents be reclassified "secret" and that a check be made to insure that no distribution has inadvertantly been made to the Department of Commerce, or other off-Project personnel or agencies.

2. These instructions do not pertain to documents regarding clinical or therapeutic uses of radioisotopes and similar materials beneficial to human disorders and diseases.

ATOMIC ENERGY COMMISSION

O. G. HAYWOOD, JR.
Colonel, Corps of Engineers.

RESTRICTED DATA

CLASSIFICATION CANCELLED
AUTHORITY: DOE/SA-20
BY H.R. SCHMIDT, DATE:
HR Schmidt 2/22/94

SECRET

Exhibit 6-1

Author's Notes: Turner's book is suggested reading for the investigative buff.

/-/-/-/-/-/-/-/-/-/

Of course, the possibility that Oswald was hypoprogrammed raises all sorts of questions and conjecture. In-as-much as I don't know who could have done it, I can only offer the reader some information so that you can draw your own conclusions. For example, we know that Oswald renounced his U.S. citizenship when he "defected" to the Soviet Union. We know that he was there long enough to find work and get married. Logic suggests that the GRU, the Soviet Intelligence Agency responsible for internal security, found him a job so that they could keep track of him.

When he returned to the United States, I believe that we can assume that (by that time) he was well known to the KGB, the FBI and the CIA. There are also suggestions that he was an informant of both the FBI and the CIA. Then, there is George DeMohrenschildt, a well-educated, successful Soviet businessman, who, for no apparent reason (i.e.: Having nothing in common with) attached himself to the Oswalds offering them his friendship and financial aid. Why? The answer that has been suggested by many authors is that DeMohrenschildt was a KGB agent. I submit that it is more likely that DeMohrenschildt was a CIA agent. Again, "why"? From all accounts, the KGB had no interest in Oswald.

Author's Notes: I don't remember where I heard, or saw, that when Oswald defected to the Soviet Union, he was "debriefed" by the KGB. This means that he was interviewed by the KGB to see what intelligence information Oswald possessed and of what value. They determined that Oswald knew nothing "of interest" to the KGB. (Oswald had been stationed in Atsugi, Japan, which "housed" the U-2)

/-/-/-/-/-/-/-/-/

If the KGB had no interest in Oswald, the CIA did. If it were not so, why would the agency maintain a file on him?

However, I do not for a moment, believe that the CIA as an agency of the United States Government, was responsible for the assassination of President Kennedy. That does not preclude individuals with CIA "credentials" from plotting to kill the President. My "person of interest" (as we shall discover in the next chapter) did have those credentials.

I have tried hard to avoid getting into the Oswald "lone killer" debate. However, *any* discussion of the assassination must include Oswald. My reason being is that I am confident that he was a player in the conspiracy; a "patsy" if you will. For example, the weapon that is alleged to have fired the fatal shots, the Mannlicher-Carcano 6.25 rifle, a weapon from the 19th Century, has been proven by weapons experts, that it lacked the accuracy to hit its "target" from the distance it was supposed to have been fired from. On the other hand, a Mauser Rifle 7.65 alleged to have been found in the Depository, did have that accuracy! The former rifle was probably never used as a sniper weapon whereas the latter was! There are some interesting aspects of the Mauser which merit special attention:

> "The Mauser rifle in various forms and state of development was very widely sold to Spain, Turkey, Belgium, Argentina, Chile, and Greece amongst many other countries. No longer in production. In service with several emergent countries and *also with various guerilla bodies.*"
>
> —Janes Book of Weapons (1975)

The muzzle velocity was approximately 2,400 foot per second and which the rate of fire was from 10-15 rounds a minute. Roughly speaking, this is about four to six seconds per round in the hands of an expert.

Chapter Seven

That the author's "person of interest" is one who had motive, access, and the resources to assassinate the President.

"The appearance and reappearance of "dark-skinned", Spanish-looking or "Negro" men in the descriptions of the witnesses intrigued me. Not only was the man in the lair identified this way, but the "epileptic" observed in Dealy Plaza was described as a Latin man wearing Army green combat carb.

—Jim Garrison in "On The Trail of The Assassins"

Reference the quote of Jim Garrison, the much maligned author of "On The Trail . . .", he surmised that those "dark skinned" men were Cuban exiles. However, I am suggesting that they could have just as easily have been Filipino Scouts. After all, Garrison had no reason (as I have) to believe otherwise. I am also suggesting that a Filipino would be more dark-skinned Negro in appearance than the average Cuban. As you might imagine, this was a critical piece of evidence for me as far as substantiating the Scout's claim.

The question now is where do I begin to unveil the name of my "person of interest"? Before I do that, I want to go to Walt Brown's *Treachery In Dallas.* (Re: 64) Where he begins, in his Prologue by asking the following questions:

1. Who was of a strong enough right-wing philosophy?
2. Who had the necessary sniper/weapons skill?
3. Who could blend into the scenery of Dallas, Texas, at high noon during a highly visible presidential motorcade and have no notice taken of them?
4. Who was in a position where they could not, under any circumstances, be investigated in any serious way by the local police?
5. Who could make all decisions as to whom was arrested?
6. Who could see to it that the lone suspect, and hence the case, would never make it to a courtroom where both sides of the issue could be presented?

His answer was: *the local police!*

Here again, I would, as in the case of blaming the CIA *per se,* not blame the entire Dallas Police Department for the assassination.

I cannot believe that after all of these years, someone in that department would not have come forward and admitted to the conspiracy. What I will now do is answer Brown's questions with my own thoughts.

Question #1. Who was of a strong enough right-wing philosophy?
Answer: Any "warhawk" on Cuba or Vietnam
Question #2. Who had the necessary sniper/weapons of skill?
Answer: The Filipino Scout

Re: 64 Treachery In Dallas by Walt Brown, Carroll & Graf Inc. (pg. 9)

Question #3. Who could blend into the scenery of Dallas, Texas, at high noon during a highly visible presidential motorcade and have no notice taken of them?
Answer: The Filipino Scout
Question #4. Who was in a position where they could not, under any circumstances, be investigated in any serious way by the local police?
Answer: Anyone representing himself as an individual with the FBI or CIA and whose authority was unquestioned.
Question #5. Who could make all decisions as to whom was arrested?
Answer: That same individual.
Question #6. Who could see to it that the lone suspect, and hence the case, would never make it to a courtroom where both sides of the issue could be presented?
Answer: That same individual.

Author's Notes: I believe that my answers to questions 4 thru 6 are absolutely on target. Why? Because when I was on duty with the Army as a Special Agent, Counterintelligence, I had no problem with local law enforcement agencies. Their cooperation in conjunction with any request that I made was never denied me.

/-/-/-/-/-/-/-/-/

Now, I will name my "person of interest"; a person of influence, reputation as an American hero; a person with a possible motive, and the resources in terms of power and personnel, *General Edward G. Lansdale!*

So, what kind of a man was Lansdale? I begin with a passage out of *President Kennedy: Profile of Power* by Richard Reeves. (Re: 65)

> "Back at the State Department, Rusk asked J. Graham Persons, Assistant Secretary of State for the Far East, what he knew about Lansdale. Notes on the conversation indicate that Persons told Rusk that Lansdale performed ably in Manila; was close to Diem; was a lonewolf; tagged as an operator; flamboyant and not a team player".

As the story goes, the President had asked Lansdale if Rusk had told him that "I'd like you to go over to Vietnam as our ambassador?" (Continuing) . . . Mr.

Rusk certainly had not, and was appalled at the idea of the CIA's best known agent in Asia representing the State Department." (Re: 66)

Author's Notes: For a biographical clip of Lansdale see Annex A.

/-/-/-/-/-/-/-/-/

Now to the questions posed by Walt Brown (Treachery In Dallas):

With respect to Question #1: Who was of a strong enough right-wing philosophy? While there are many in this category, I believe that Lansdale was high in that list. He was a "warhawk" on getting rid of Castro; a "warhawk" on winning the war in Vietnam. Would he kill for what he believed in as a just cause? I believe that his actions in the Philippines and Vietnam. Would he kill for what he believed was a just cause? I believe that his actions in the Philippines and Vietnam bear that belief out. However, with due respect, any soldier will and does kill for his country.

Question #2: Who had the necessary sniper/weapons of skill? Of course, the Filipino Scouts had the reputation and demonstrated their skill as snipers; there were none better!

Question #3: Who could blend into the scenery of Dallas, Texas, at high noon during a highly visible presidential motorcade and have no notice taken of them? Of course, *any* individual of Negroid or Hispanic culture could have.

Question #4: Who was in a position where they could not, under any circumstances, be investigated in any serious way by the local police? Lansdale could! Lansdale, as a "flamboyant" operator could easily convince local police that he had the full faith and power of the Federal Government behind him.

Question #5: Who could make all decisions as to whom was arrested? Here again, Lansdale could! Keep in mind that the "Patsy" (Oswald) had *already* been selected (i.e.: Prior to the actual assassination!)

Re: 65 President Kennedy: Profile of Power, by Richard Reeves, Simon & Schuster (1993) pg. 50

Re: 66 Ibid pg. 49

Question #6: Who could see to it that the lone suspect, and hence the case, would never make it to a courtroom where both sides of the issue could be presented? Here again, only someone with daring, power, and influence could have done that; Lansdale for example.

Well, there you have it. In writing this book, it was not with the intention of demeaning General Lansdale. After all, he was an American icon; no less than three books were written based on his exploits and daring. However, the truth is the truth. I call Lansdale a "person of interest" because he had motive and the resources to carry out the planning and execution of the President. In addition, he was placed in Dealy Plaza on the day of the assassination. I quote a passage from *Plausible Denial* by Mark Lane (Re 67):

> "When Prouty and I had lunch on Capitol Hill during June 1991,
> he showed me a photograph that had been taken in Dallas that day.
> It displayed a man striding away from the camera at an angle and
> therefore provided only a right side-back view. "There is no doubt
> in my mind that's Ed Lansdale."

Author's Notes: L. Fletcher Prouty, Colonel, USAF (Ret) served as Chief, Special Operations, to Joint Chiefs of Staff during the Kennedy presidency. His special assignment was to support the world-wide clandestine activities of the CIA.

/-/-/-/-/-/-/-/-/

What about Lansdale's connection to the Filipinos?

Right after WWII, the communists threatened to take over the Philippines. Lansdale, as an agent of the CIA, was sent there to help establish a government that would be friendly to the U.S. Lansdale did so; recruiting former soldiers and scouts and fighting a counterinsurgency war with an army paid for by the CIA, Lansdale was successful.

As a result, Lansdale established and maintained a close, personal relationship with certain members of the Filipino Army.

The *same* army that Lansdale had used to position Magsaysay as President of the Philippines.

Re: 67 *Plausible Denial* by Mark Lane, Thunder's Mouth Press (1991) (pg. 103)

Members of the *same* army Lansdale recruited to help move over a million North Vietnamese into the south across the 17th Parallel (The Geneva Conference of 1954, divided Indochina into half. North of the parallel was to be the Democratic Republic of Vietnam. South of the 17th was to be the "State of Vietnam")

The *same* army members, Filipino soldiers (and/or scouts) who were now, by definition, mercenaries, paid by the CIA and under the command of General Lansdale (The CIA's Army!)

Lansdale and the Saigon Military Mission (SMM) established the CIA's man, Diem, as President of South Vietnam. As such, Lansdale became a close personal friend of Diem.

Lansdale and the CIA were part of the "Diem-must-stay" camp.

For someone to conspire to, or commit murder, there must first be proven that they had a motive. I'll mention three common reasons: *revenge*, to protect one's family, himself, or his country, and three, for money. For the soldier on the field of battle it is self-preservation and to protect his country from its enemies. One of the most common reasons (I believe) is for revenge. Which of these do you think would motivate a man such as General Lansdale to commit or cause to be committed? In my mind the motive, first and foremost was revenge. Another might have been, and perhaps a little far-fetched, was to protect his country *or another country—South Vietnam!* If Lansdale knew that the President intended to remove all troops from Vietnam after his reelection in 1964, Lansdale might have reasoned that it would spell the end of a nation which he had, almost single-handedly created, that would be a motive.

If Lansdale believed (and I believe he did) that President Kennedy authorized the assassination of Diem, a close personal friend of his and the man that he, Lansdale had struggled so hard to install as South Vietnam's President, that would be motive (revenge). Remember Diem was assassinated on the 22nd of November, *just three weeks later*. (Can anyone else see a connection between the two assassinations other than myself?)

If Lansdale harbored any resentment and sense of abandonment when he was not sent to Saigon as America's first ambassador to South Vietnam after Kennedy had personally told him that he would be; that could be a motive.

If Lansdale believed that Kennedy was responsible for the Bay of Pigs fiasco, that could be a motive.

If Lansdale believed that Kennedy, after the 1964 election, intended to dismantle the CIA; that could be a motive. Kennedy *did* terminate the MONGOOSE Operation in which Lansdale was in charge. Kennedy also scrapped Lansdale's counterinsurgency plan for the liberation of Cuba. That could be a motive.

If Lansdale thought that Kennedy was going to pursue a policy of détente with the Soviet Union after the 1964 election. That could be a motive.

While any one of the previous motives by themselves, could be dismissed as pure speculation, I suggest that all of them, piled on top of each other could have caused the General to "snap".

What I have hoped to have shown in this book is that Lansdale *had* a motive; he had access i.e.: The freedom to move about unfettered (and he was placed at the scene by Prouty on the day of the assassination), and he had the resources (the Filipino Scouts) to commit the act. Therefore, there is ample reason to identify him as a "person of interest"; a person definitely a candidate for further questioning.

ANNEX A

(Biographical Sketch of General Lansdale)

Biographical Sketch of Maj. Gen. Lansdale (Re: 68)

Born in 1908, a U.S. Army Officer who became a clandestine operative in the Philippines and Vietnam and a key figure in the backstage campaign to topple Fidel Castro's regime in Cuba. In 1943, he was commissioned as a first lieutenant and assigned to the San Francisco field office of the Army's Military Intelligence Service. Soon after, he was recruited by the Office of Strategic Services (OSS). During WWII, most of Lansdale's duties involved writing OSS training manuals and gathering basic intelligence information.

In 1949, he was assigned to the Office of Policy Coordination, the highly secret covert action organization run by Frank Wisner. In Washington, D.C., he met Ramon Magasaysay, a member of the Filipino Congress, and mapped out a way to make him an anti-HUK president of the Philippines. In 1953, Magasaysay won a landslide victory launching Lansdale's reputation as America's expert in beating communist guerrillas. In beating the HUKs, Lansdale used bizarre tactics, such as spreading rumors that a local vampire was pursuing HUKs and then having anit-HUK units kill HUKs by puncturing their throats and draining their blood.

Lansdale backed Ngo Dinh Diem, a former French colonial functionary, to be president of South Vietnam. Lansdale also conceived of the idea of a propaganda campaign to get nearly one million Catholics in the north to migrate south. Having set up Diem as the American-approved President of South Vietnam, Lansdale returned to Washington where he became a major advisor on special operations; his job essentially gave him control over military support for CIA covert operations.

After the abortive Bay of Pigs invasion, the Kennedy administration began operation MONGOOSE, an intensive covert action campaign against Cuba, and had the CIA develop plans to assassinate Castro, in which Lansdale was a major player. The Cuban Missile crisis ended MONGOOSE and Lansdale was soon on his way to Venezuela and Bolivia to inspect anti-guerrilla activity. He retired in 1963.

Re: 68   *The Encyclopedia of Espionage* by Norman Polmar & Thomas Allen (1997), Gramercy Books (pgs. 328-300)

ANNEX B

(Memorandum On Conference With The President, 18 March 1960)

March 18, 1960

MEMORANDUM OF CONFERENCE WITH THE PRESIDENT
2:30 PM, March 17, 1960

Others present: Vice President Nixon, Secretary Herter,
Mr. Merchant, Mr. Rubottom, Secretary Anderson,
Secretary Irwin, Admiral Burke, Mr. Allen Dulles,
Mr. Richard Bissell, Colonel J. C. King, Gordon
Gray, Major Eisenhower, General Goodpaster

After Mr. Herter gave a brief comment concerning use of the OAS
in connection with the Cuban situation, Mr. Allen Dulles reported
to the President an action plan provided by the "5412" group for
covert operations to effect a change in Cuba.   The first step
will be to form a moderate opposition group in exile.   This will
take about one month.   Its slogan will be to "restore the revolution" which Castro has betrayed.   A medium wave radio station
to carry out gray or black broadcasts into Cuba will be established, probably on Swan Island (south of Cuba, belonging to the
United States), in two months.   Concurrently a network of dis-
affected elements will be established within Cuba.

To a question by the President Mr. Bissell indicated the opposition would probably be located in Puerto Rico.   Mexico would
be better if they could be brought to agree, which is not likely.
Venezuela would be even better, but it is not probable that the
government could permit this.   Mr. Rubottom thought Costa
Rica may be a possibility and this will be explored.

Mr. Allen Dulles said that preparations of a para-military force
will begin outside of Cuba, the first stage being to get a cadre
of leaders together for training.   The formation of this force
might take something like eight months.

The President said that he knows of no better plan for dealing
with this situation.   The great problem is leakage and breach
of security.   Everyone must be prepared to swear that he has not

heard of it.   He said we should limit American contacts with
the groups involved to two or three people, getting Cubans
to do most of what must be done.   Mr. Allen Dulles said that a
group of New York businessmen is being organized as cover for
this activity.   The President indicated some question about
this, and reiterated that there should be only two or three
governmental people connected with this in any way.   He understood that the effort will be to undermine Castro's position and
prestige.   Mr. Bissell commented that the opposition group
would undertake a money-raising campaign to obtain funds on
their own -- in the United States, Cuba and elsewhere.

Mr. Gray commented that events may occur rapidly in Cuba,
and force our hand before these preparations are completed.

Secretary Anderson stated that Castro is in reality financing
his operations out of the funds of the U. S. companies that are
operating in Cuba.   He suggested that the Administration might
take steps to bring business leaders together with elements
of our government to consider what course the businesses --
which are now being milked of their assets -- should take.   He
said he had received a report that Castro is trying to inflame
Cuban opinion and create an incident against the Americans
which would touch off attacks on Americans in Cuba which might
result in the death of thousands.   The President stated that
once the operation Mr. Douglas had proposed gets started, there
will be great danger to the Americans in Cuba.   Mr. Rubottom
said that the "warning phase" of our evacuation plan is already
in effect, and that many Americans are leaving, with almost
no new ones going in.

Mr. Anderson said he thought that if we were to cut the Cubans
off from their fuel supply, the effect would be devastating on
them within a month or six weeks.   There is some question
whether other countries would join in denying fuel oil -- especially
Venezuela.   Mr. Anderson added that if Cuba is to seize the
Nicaro plant or other U. S. Government property, we could not
stand on the sidelines.   In reponse to a question by the President,
it was brought out that there is no treaty on this, and that Cuba
of course has the right to confiscate the plant so long as compensation is given.   Mr. Rubottom stated that if we wanted to cut

their trade drastically we could denounce our two trade agreements with them. This would of course cut into the sales by our manufacturers to the Cubans. Mr. Nixon asked what we are doing with regard to cutting off new capital, pulling out private firms and cutting off tourism. Mr. Rubottom said that much of this is occurring of its own accord.

The President told Mr. Dulles he thought he should go ahead with the plan and the operations. He and the other agencies involved should take account of all likely Cuban reactions and prepare the actions that we would take in response to these. Mr. Irwin said the main Defense concern is how we would get our people out. We have contingency planning, but it would involve military action. The President said he would like some ground work laid with the OAS to let the Latin American countries know that if the Cubans were to start to attack our people in Cuba we would be obliged to take action.

Mr. Allen Dulles returned to the point made by Mr. Anderson -- that American business in Cuba wants guidance. The President said we should be very careful about giving this. Essentially they will have to make their own decisions. Admiral Burke stated that many of the American firms want to pull out, but do not want to endanger their people who are there. Mr. Nixon said he thought we should encourage them to come out. Particularly if they think they should get out and are simply staying there to help the U. S. Government, we should disillusion them on that score immediately.

The President said that at the next meeting he would want to know what is the sequence of events by which we see the situation developing -- specifically what actions are we to take. He said our hand should not show in anything that is done. In the meantime, State should be working on what we can do in and out of the OAS. Mr. Nixon asked Mr. Herter whether support was developing satisfactorily within the OAS. Mr. Rubottom's answer indicated that the situation is not clear. The President said that, as he saw it, Castro the Revolutionary had gained great prestige in Latin America. Castro the Politician running the government is now losing it rapidly. However, governments elsewhere cannot

oppose him too strongly since they are shaky with respect to
the potentials of action by the mobs within their own countries
to whom Castro's brand of demagoguery appeals. Essentially
the job is to get the OAS to support us.

Mr. Gray asked whether OAS support will only be forthcoming
if the Cubans actually attack Americans on the island. Mr.
Rubottom thought that the OAS might be brought to act prior to
such an attack on the basis of Castro being tied up with international communism. The President asked whether we have
to base it on the word "communism" or whether we couldn't
base it on dictatorship, confiscation, threats to life, etc. Mr.
Nixon said he thought the Caracas Resolution was based on the
term "international communism."

Mr. Bissell said he understood the sense of the meeting to be
that work could start on forming the opposition Council and on
other preparations. Mr. Herter said that the radio station is
very important. The President asked that we try to obscure the
location of the radio station.

A. J. Goodpaster
Brigadier General, USA

I wish to express my thanks and appreciation to the Eisenhower and Kennedy Libraries and to the Maryknoll Fathers and Brothers Archives for their cooperation in providing me documents included in the book. Also, to those who encouraged me over the years to complete it.

—Dr. Frank R. Durr